"Brutal honest wr[...]
Shirlee has done great justice to his memory—to John, Dick, and all the family…He would have nodded his head in agreement."
V. Marais, International Relations

"Shirlee wrote the most absorbing, painful, and hope-filled book…a spiritual journey of self-reflection, loving outreach, perseverance, and Christ hope."
P. Linnen, STJ/ACCL Liaison

"A heart-rending story…coherent and gripping. The attention to detail, including the search for medical help—and sleep—is remarkable!"
H. Barlow, PhD/Author

are you Feeding me Poison?

are you Feeding me Poison?

Shirlee Gentles

TATE PUBLISHING
AND ENTERPRISES, LLC

Are You Feeding Me Poison?
Copyright © 2012 by Shirlee Gentles. All rights reserved.

No part of this publication may be reproduced, stored in a retrieval system or transmitted in any way by any means, electronic, mechanical, photocopy, recording or otherwise without the prior permission of the author except as provided by USA copyright law.

The opinions expressed by the author are not necessarily those of Tate Publishing, LLC.

Published by Tate Publishing & Enterprises, LLC
127 E. Trade Center Terrace | Mustang, Oklahoma 73064 USA
1.888.361.9473 | www.tatepublishing.com

Tate Publishing is committed to excellence in the publishing industry. The company reflects the philosophy established by the founders, based on Psalm 68:11,
"The Lord gave the word and great was the company of those who published it."

Book design copyright © 2012 by Tate Publishing, LLC. All rights reserved.
Cover design by Allen Jomoc
Interior design by Jan Sunday Quilaquil

Published in the United States of America

ISBN: 978-1-62147-310-7
1. Biography & Autobiography: Personal Memoirs
2. Psychology: Mental Illness
12.07.24

For James. You lift me up every day. Cling to the Lord and He will guide your path

ACKNOWLEDGMENTS

For my best friend Terri. She is my rock who stood by me every step of the way. My pain was her pain. Before completing this book, Terri's beloved brother, David, lost his battle with prostate cancer. We've had a saying over our nearly forty-year friendship: "In good times and bad." However, it's apparent she's the one who's done the most giving.

For my sister Pat, who spent hours listening to me, offering encouragement and reassurance. She put her life on hold to come and stay with me following Marshall's death. She adored Marshall, too. Her love knows no bounds.

For Dr. Greg Mattingly. Without him I would not have known where to begin to find help for my son. He is a dedicated, compassionate doctor who sincerely cares for his patients. He restored Marshall's health and returned my son to me for those glorious months.

To my brother, Alan, for his comfort and genuine concern. He too was always willing to lend a sympathetic ear.

And to my brother Michael who was my sounding board, offering to read and critique my book. I appreciated his honesty, insight, and guidance. He gently insisted that I dig deep and asked me the hard questions. He also suggested that I seek publication of the book because he believed it would impact lives and help others.

For my husband, John, who found himself in the worst possible position—a no-win situation. He feels the weight of it every day of his life but always maintains a cheerful disposition and even temperament. You are my love.

For Pastors, Paul Schult, Charles Schlie, Roger Keller, Vicor Rob Biesendorfer, Beth Schult, and Greg Worzel. Thank you, thank you for your prayers, support, and especially for making Marshall's funeral so triumphant and meaningful.

Thanks to Sharon Thornton and Jamie White for introducing me to the tranquil and disciplined practice of Yoga and Meditation. Thank you for the breathe rock and for emphasizing the importance of "practicing an attitude of gratitude."

A special thanks to our treasured friends of nearly forty years, Jean and Terry Niehaus. Thank you for your love, support, and friendship.

For my mom, my friend, and exercise buddy, who's still going strong at age ninety.

And I'll be forever indebted to Richard Ivy. When every door closed on me, one man made such a difference. Every returning veteran from the armed forces deserves to have a Richard Ivy in their corner. An advocate and a self-thinker who saw the injustice of Marshall's discharge status and boldly took the initiative to delve in and examine all the facts. A real humanitarian and a credit to the VA, he was promoted to Program Analyst/Benefit Assistance Services and currently works at the VA's Washington, DC office.

TABLE OF CONTENTS

Marshall's Father 9
9/11 15
Missing 25
Deserter 29
Miramar Brig 39
Marshall's Visit 47
Anxiety/Panic 53
Coming Home 57
Self-Help 63
Are You Feeding
Me Poison? 65
Manic/Psychotic 73
Involuntary Confinement 91
Honorable
Discharge 101
Last Photo 115
Slipping Away 123
Tragedy 129
Trauma 139
Dishonorable 145
Blame 173
Guilt, Denial 181
Letting Go 195

PREFACE

More than 50 million Americans suffer from a form of mental illness. It is estimated that about 2.5 to 4 percent of all Americans suffer from bipolar disorder, with about fifty-five thousand new cases diagnosed each year. To put that into perspective, ten out of three hundred high school classmates have the illness. Bipolar affects your neighbor, your brother, and your cousin. No one is immune. It takes a toll on your own personal health as well as a devastating toll on family and friends. Bipolar is an illness, not a weakness, and should be treated as such. Yet the system is flawed, and there are many gaps in treatment across the board. First, it's an illness that is hard for the sufferer to recognize. Next, it is still widely undiagnosed and most insurance companies do not cover the costs for treatment. Many healthcare professionals are inexperienced in treating the disorder and sometimes agree with the patient who thinks they no longer need to take their medication, the ramifications of which have disastrous consequences, akin to someone suffering from diabetes that goes off his insulin, stopping seizure medication for an epileptic, or the discontinuation of heart drugs for those who suffer from heart disease. The analogies are too numerous to mention. But these illnesses are tangible whereas with bipolar, it's just the brain. Bipolar disorder is so prevalent that the play *Next to Normal* was written about it. And yet, funding is so inadequate. As a matter of fact, mental health funds are being cut nationwide.

That's not to say there aren't wonderful organizations

out there, more notably NAMI (National Association of Mental Illness) and BringChange2Mind. The latter's philosophy is "Strength in numbers" and "*Do Not* tolerate the stigma of mental health." It was founded by Glenn Close whose sister and nephew were diagnosed with bipolar disorder. How I wish I'd heard of this organization sooner, because I know with certainty that my son did feel very alone.

A former navy seal and author of *The Heart and the Fist*, Eric Greitens started the non-profit organization www.themissioncontinues.org in 2007, which brings together post 9/11 veterans, civilians, and active-duty volunteers in service to our country through service to their community. He started this organization after interviewing returning wounded or disabled veterans and found their universal desire was to return to active duty. This is what my son mentioned to me over and over again—his desire to return to active duty. Marshall would have benefited greatly if he felt like he was contributing to society while working alongside fellow veterans.

I decided to share my heartfelt story in an effort to highlight the needs of those who suffer from a mental disorder. This was not an easy story to write, and it took me almost four years to find the courage to do so. I want to pay tribute to my son Marshall who even when he was sick made me proud of him every day of his life. He was the brave one, not me.

MARSHALL'S FATHER

My ex-husband Dick died on April 7, 2010. Whatever the official cause of death is, Dick died of a broken heart.

His death came just two years after we lost our son Marshall. He died a profoundly sad and lonely man. He was discovered collapsed on his bedroom floor by his on again/off again girlfriend a few shorts weeks after his fifty-ninth birthday. He and I spoke infrequently after our son's death. Any trace of our earlier happy years together—the wedding, the joyous occasion of the birth of our son—were now gone forever. Our amicable cooperation after our divorce, in the interests of our son, ceased. Our conversations had become short, cordial monotones.

Dick was never able to cope with the loss of our son. He told me, "You have a reason to carry on. You have James. I have nothing." I once tried to encourage him to become more involved with his niece's two children. I knew the pep talk was futile. He said, "Yes, I know, but it's not the same. They have a father." Our relationship deteriorated to the point that he never even informed me when his sister Kathy died from ovarian cancer in 2009. Not even aware that she was sick, news of her death came as a shock to me. Kathy and I had remained in contact after Dick and I divorced. She was crazy about Marshall, and we wrote often over the years, exchanging photos of our kids. She attended Marshall's graduation from the naval academy in Great Lakes and wrote to him often.

She ended each and every phone call and letter with the exact same words, "Love and God bless." I didn't grasp the full meaning of her words at the time. I was at best a lukewarm Christian, having converted to the Lutheran faith to marry Dick at their Immanuel Lutheran Church in Dundee, Illinois. Her words impact me now, though. I understand their meaning and know of the sincerity with which they were spoken.

Sadly, Kathy and I became estranged not long after Marshall's death. Losing her friendship was a crushing blow. I'd held out hope and even assumed that inevitably we'd reconcile. I envisioned us hugging at Marshall's graveside. I had naively pictured this same scenario with Dick, hoping we'd all grieve together the loss of our beautiful Marshall. But neither came to pass.

For the life of him, Dick could not understand why I stayed with John, the man he blamed for Marshall's death. Since he wasn't there that night to witness the horror, he was unable to grasp the full depth of the danger, the surreal events that changed all of our lives.

When I search the eyes of strangers, I sense that many of them too may have suffered from the loss of a loved one or have suffered a life-changing event. To lose a parent, sibling, or child is inevitable, and yet with the loss of Marshall at age twenty-six, I sometimes feel my loss trumps all others. No doubt selfish of me. Yet, I still fall asleep at night, giving thanks to God for all my blessings—my health, my kids, my vibrant ninety-year-old mother who is still with us. I pray for the healing of others—my girlfriend's husband with myasthenia gravis, her brother who just lost his battle with prostate cancer, and a friend whose son is in prison. My nightly prayer is ever-changing, but gratitude is the constant denominator. Still, the sadness seems ever present, and at times I struggle to keep it from weighing me down. Often, the circumstances of Marshall's death or a bizarre statement he made in the past comes back to haunt me. For instance, I find myself on occasion suddenly and involuntarily blurting out the word *no*. I have, on occasion, gotten a quizzical glance from someone. When this happens, it jolts me back to reality, and I pretend to be singing the words to a song.

But hearing of Dick's death was a shock. He had no health concerns of which I was aware. He was, however, a heavy beer drinker most of his life. This was the most significant contributing factor that led to our divorce years earlier. I often wondered what our lives would have been like if Dick wasn't an alcoholic. Once he started drinking, I knew he wouldn't stop until he passed out. I used to plead with him to get help to overcome his addiction. I told him on numerous occasions that drinking in front of Marshall was a bad influence. Wherever we went I was the designated driver. I would watch him from across the room at family gatherings as he degenerated into a glossy-eyed and inebriated state. It became a lonely and predictable existence. His drinking took its toll on our marriage. When I came home from my job at Jewel Foods late at night, he and his buddy had their empty beer bottles lined up on the porch ledge, in plain view of passing cars on our very busy street. This caused me as much embarrassment as it did anger. I asked where Marshall was while he and his friend were drinking. It was evident that the beer drinking started from the moment I left for work in the late afternoon. When I gave him the ultimatum, I already knew alcohol would win out over me. The day I left Dick, I handed him the phone number for Alcoholics Anonymous. He never admitted he had a problem, though, and I never stopped caring for him or feeling sorry for him.

But I was determined that Marshall would not suffer from his parent's divorce. Marshall was only four years old when our marriage ended in 1985. Dick and I remained friends, and although I had custody of Marshall, there was never the all-too-common power struggle over visitation. Marshall spent most major holidays with his dad as well as every summer. Dick and I would meet in Bloomington, Illinois, which was the halfway point. Over the years we lost count of the numerous times we'd meet there, always taking time to have lunch together and catch-up. We made sure to praise each other's parenting in front of Marshall. We parted every time with a genuine hug and optimism for a "great time!" I truly believe Marshall thrived knowing that we not only loved him but cared for each other. I knew that while Dick worked, Marshall was in good hands with his Aunt Kathy. As a preschool teacher at Immanuel Lutheran, she not only loved Marshall but had patience and compassion. My sister Pat lived close to Dick and would oftentimes pick up Marshall to spend time with him also. Over the years Dick and Marshall were like two peas in a pod. They bonded over the restoration of numerous classic cars and motorcycles, acquiring parts at swap meets and flea markets.

Dick's death came as a shock to my husband John, too. I got the phone call at 1:00 a.m. from a mutual friend of ours. By the time I got off the phone and returned to bed, it was after 2:00 a.m. It was then that I told John that Dick had died. With disbelief, he blurted out, "Dick Fink?" When I confirmed this he said "Oh no," and sounded quite distressed.

I left the next morning to drive up to my sister Pat's house near Dundee with the intention of going to Dick's funeral. I spoke with John a couple of times while I was away, each time detecting a remorseful tone in his voice. I knew he felt somewhat responsible for Dick's untimely death. There's no doubt in my mind that the sadness, grief, and stress that Dick experienced with the loss of his son contributed to and facilitated his death. Dealing with my own shock and sadness over this news, I was incapable of offering reassurance to John. I knew his actions the night of Marshall's death, however justified, have consequences and repercussions. I let him take his lumps alone.

9/11

There was a defining moment in my life when I knew for certain that my child, who I loved more than anything in this world, was profoundly ill. It was both chilling and terrifying. It came in the form of a question. His words will haunt me forever. Like a Cheshire cat, he slowly turned his face to within inches of my own. Without the slightest hint of humor, his psychotic eyes searching mine for an honest answer, he urgently asked me, "Are you feeding me poison?"

While he watched me intently to see if I acted guilty so he could confirm his suspicions, I very calmly told him, "No, Marshall, I would never do that. Please don't ask me that again." All the while my heart was pounding, my mind was racing, and I was nauseated with fear.

Marshall was born on August 11, 1981. He was diagnosed with bipolar disorder in September 2005. He died on January 11, 2008, at age twenty-six.

After my son's death, people would say to me, "You're so strong." Well, I don't feel strong, and the toll my son's illness took on my own health is something I am aware of daily and take pains to mitigate. Sometimes I sit in his very quiet bedroom, although I do this less frequently now, and have a good cry. I remember the countless times I cleaned this room and tidied it up. Now, except for occasional dusting, it never needs tidying. The tangible proof of losing a child is especially evident in his bedroom. Once chaotic at times and overcrowded with friends, that same bedroom now remains perfect and perfectly quiet. I cry just writing these words.

Until the day I received a call in September 2005 from a doctor at the Naval Medical Center in San Diego where Marshall was stationed, I thought everything was fine. Marshall had served nearly four years in the navy. Prior to this, he had been rather adrift after high school, unsure of his career path. But, he had found his niche and excelled right from the start. We spoke on the phone regularly, and his dad had just spent two weeks with him in June that same year. They took a road trip together in the southwest and had a wonderful time. Dick later stated that Marshall never showed signs of a mental disorder.

- - - - - - - - - - -

I remarried in 1990. Marshall was close in age to his new stepsisters, Heather and Allison. When the girls stayed with us on the weekends, we went to the local attractions—the park, the zoo, float trips, the pool, water parks, Six Flags, and Purina Farms. Our son James was born in 1995 when Marshall was fourteen. Our blended family was happy, and the older siblings doted on their new little brother. Years later, it would be Marshall's stepsister Heather who would write the glowing tribute to Marshall that was printed on his memorial bulletin.

After Marshall's high school graduation, he went to stay at his father's for an extended visit. Their passion of restoring cars and motorcycles continued in earnest. They always had a project they were working on. Marshall was easygoing, trusting, loving, affectionate, and considerate. These were happy, carefree times spent with his dad.

Then the horrible tragedy on September 11, 2001, shocked the nation. Terrorists flew two passenger planes into the World Trade Center and one into the Pentagon. A fourth plane did not reach its intended target when a few brave passengers rushed the terrorists. Tragically, that plane crashed into a field, killing all on board.

It was immediately after 9/11, and with a surging feeling of patriotism, that Marshall enlisted in the navy. We were so very proud of him. He was twenty. Boot camp was a cinch, and he excelled in his specialty courses. On March 22, 2002, he was filled with excitement at his graduation in basic training from the naval academy in Great Lakes, Illinois. It was only natural that he would become an Engineman on the USS *Peleliu* in San Diego. With all the restorations he and his dad did on car engines prior to entering the military, this was the perfect fit.

In 2003, my husband and I along with our two daughters and young son set out on a road trip across the country with the destination of San Diego to see Marshall. We took in the sights that included Disneyland and California Adventure. Marshall was so happy and proud to show us his ship and take us for a tour inside. He beamed with pride while showing us the engine room, his bunk, and the ship's anchor. He enthusiastically told us about his recent deployment to the Gulf when the USS *Peleliu* delivered US Marines into Afghanistan. Our Christmas card that year showed all six of us standing in front of his ship. It was truly a memorable family experience with all of our children enjoying themselves, and one another. I snapped a photo of Marshall at a rare moment when he was standing alone. He looked so handsome, relaxed, proud, and happy.

In January 2005, Marshall's paternal grandmother died, and he took a leave to attend the funeral. Having remained very close to my ex-mother-in-law, I also attended her funeral along with our younger son James. Marshall and his brother were inseparable that day, as was always the case when the two of them were together. Marshall, with his father, greeted all who attended. He was gracious, shook hands, smiled, and spoke with such ease—a gift he learned from his dad, I must admit. I watched from a distance as everyone from his small hometown openly admired one of their own who chose to serve his country.

It was a tearful good-bye after the funeral. He was flying back to San Diego the next day, and I wasn't sure when I'd see him again. It was especially hard for Marshall and James to say good-bye. The two of them went to the car to be alone. Marshall told me afterward that he wanted to get James a mini-bike motorcycle someday soon but wanted my permission. I said that at age nine James was still too young. I told him that I would keep an open mind for the future, however. If only I had known that this would be the last time I would ever see the old Marshall again.

Marshall was by now an electrician's mate second class (EM2) and an engineman third class. He was scheduled to be deployed to the Gulf a second time sometime in July. In June, his father flew out to San Diego, and the two of them went on another road trip to Arizona. I spoke with the two of them a couple times, and they were having a good time together. John and I talked to Marshall several times that summer.

But Marshall deteriorated quickly after that—sometime between late July and mid-September. In one particular call, he sounded frustrated when telling us the navy wouldn't be sending him overseas after all. He stated that a fellow seaman, who was married and had a child, needed the additional income that the military paid when one was deployed. He said he was going to let this buddy go instead of him, but I could hear the aggravation in his voice. He had been preparing for this deployment and was looking forward to it. He called again on my birthday, August 10, but it was a short call. He sounded overwhelmed, preoccupied, and even a little anxious, which worried me a bit. He stated he had so much to do, and so many things he wanted to get rid of. He had been accumulating motorcycle parts that he decided to sell, along with a couple of motorcycles, specifically his older 1960 Triumph, a fairly rare and valuable bike. He and his dad did this often—buy a bike at a bargain price, clean it up and get it running, and then sell it for a profit. He now had a couple of storage units in which he kept all of these possessions, and it sounded to me like he was overwhelmed with too much responsibility. I thought it was a good idea, also, that he should sell these possessions and simplify his life.

Then on September 22, 2005, our lives changed forever. I received a call from a Dr. K. from the Naval Medical Center in San Diego. He told me that Marshall had been admitted there after exhibiting "uncharacteristic and unacceptable behavior." He was insubordinate and aggressive and had recently dropped twenty pounds. He had grandiose ideas and would go off on a tangent, speaking out of line. The doctor's next statement sent shockwaves through me. He stated that Marshall's behavior was consistent with bipolar disorder. I had heard of this illness, but now I tried to remember what I knew about it. I asked a lot of questions—Was he okay? Was he going to get better? Could I talk to him? He assured me that for now there was nothing I could do but that he would keep me informed of Marshall's treatment. He further stated that Marshall was in denial regarding his diagnosis. Then they put Marshall on the phone. Hoping they had made a terrible mistake, I listened intently to see if I could detect a change in his voice. I asked him if he knew why he had been admitted. He was indifferent and nonchalant. He said, "Hi, Mom. I'm just here with a little cold. I've been working too hard, and they just want me to rest." When I questioned him further, he became agitated and said, "I can't talk right now," and hung up the phone.

I immediately started to research bipolar disorder:
> A rollercoaster of moods. In the manic phase, people demonstrate extraordinary amounts of energy. They are talkative and are perpetually on the go. They make grandiose plans and often try to carry them out. At times, they might hallucinate. The manic phase is fol-

lowed by a depression so gloomy that people withdraw from interacting with others. People with manic-depression need hospitalizations only when they are out of touch with the real world. Many never need to be in a hospital.

Another article stated:

Bipolar disorder has some roots in genes, some in brain chemistry and life stresses. It's a common illness, affecting from three percent to eight percent of the population. The two poles of bipolar are emotional highs and lows. During the high periods, people need less sleep than usual. They have unbelievable reserves of energy. They are talkative and outgoing. During a high episode, people often make terrible decisions, act impulsively, and take risks that can affect their health. Thinking is disorganized, and hallucinations can develop. During periods of the other pole—depression—energy is gone. People don't want to interact socially. Concentration is difficult. Self-esteem disappears. Suicidal thoughts intrude. Brain chemistry figures greatly into bipolar disorder. Brain chemistry refers to messenger chemicals in the brain—dopamine, serotonin, and others—that activate neighboring brain cells and transmit information between brain cells. In bipolar disorder, as in many other disorders, brain chemistry is upset. Medications can often restore chemistry and keep the highs and lows on an even keel. Bipolar often strikes between the age of 17 or 18.

Over the course of several weeks, Marshall was drug tested

at least twice. The results were negative for drugs both times. I stated to the doctor that I knew Marshall would test negative for drugs since he was very health conscience. He would never take drugs. He was always working out, drank lots of water, never touched soda, and always took vitamins. He read food labels, preferring fresh unprocessed foods whenever possible. I would often send care packages to Marshall containing his requested protein powder, Muscle Milk, or whey protein from his favorite nutrition store.

Initially, doctors said he was uncooperative, refusing the anti-psychotic medication. This didn't surprise me, and I stated to the doctor that the strongest medication Marshall had ever taken was aspirin. I was told that he was cheeking his meds and trying to spit them out later. He finally cooperated when he understood that refusing the meds would result in a reprimand to his fellow naval man who was assigned the job of handing out medications to patients.

Marshall was treated by several doctors during his hospitalization at the Naval Medical Center, and I was in contact with all of them. I spoke regularly with Dr. K, Dr. E, and finally a Dr. M. Dr. M. told me Marshall's meds were being "adjusted," he was "doing great," and was "stable." It was determined that he had a mild bipolar condition, and we were reassured that his disorder required a low maintenance dose of Risperdal and Depakote. Both drugs are used in the treatment of schizophrenia and bipolar disorder, with Depakote particularly administered for the manic episodes of the bipolar disorder. I was deeply saddened when informed by Dr. M that the navy would have to discharge Marshall. I was told that the navy was not equipped to accommodate a soldier with a mental diagnosis of bipolar disease, and the next step would entail a review by a medical board, ultimately resulting in a medical discharge. Dr. M speculated the discharge would be finalized sometime in early January 2006. I knew this would be devastating news for Marshall. He was informed of this course, likely in late November.

MISSING

We purchased airfare for Marshall to come home for Christmas. He told me he was really looking forward to the trip and put in for a leave of absence. The leave was granted, and I was going to pick him up from the airport on Christmas Day, with a return flight to San Diego scheduled for January 5, 2006. Determined to outdo previous years, I pulled out an arsenal of decorations to welcome him home.

I lost contact with Marshall when on Sunday, December 11, 2005 he didn't answer his cell phone. Further repeated calls went unanswered.

I became alarmed when I received a call on Monday, December, 19, from a Petty Officer P. from the Psych Medical Hold stating that Marshall had not reported in with her as was required. She asked me if I would contact Marshall. She further stated, "No big deal. Just have him call tomorrow or the next day." I didn't mention to her at the time that I, too, was unable to reach him. My concern was growing. I began calling him in earnest, leaving messages to reemphasize how eagerly we anticipated his visit on Christmas Day. I tried calling both Dr. E and Dr. M to find out if they talked to Marshall but was unable to reach either of them.

I tried in vain to reach someone, anyone. When I did make contact with a naval man on watch, I was told that due to holiday lockdown no one was available until after the holidays. I left numerous messages for psych medical hold, in particular Petty Officer P., but no call was ever returned. I called navy info dispatch and was given a second dispatch number. A man named N. was sympathetic to my cause and suggested I call TPU, the transient personnel unit. I was suddenly thrust into navigating my way through navy jargon. No call was returned from TPU. I tried to get the phone number for the apartment complex where Marshall was living along with two other seamen who were also in the medical hold, but the phone operator would not give me the number because I didn't have the name of the leaseholder.

With nowhere else to turn, I contacted the sheriff's department in San Diego. A Deputy Sanchez agreed to go to Marshall's apartment for me. He called me back to say that although Marshall was not home, he interviewed his roommate, Travis. Deputy Sanchez said the roommate last saw Marshall on Friday morning, December 16, 2005, and hadn't seen or heard from him since. Deputy Sanchez filed a missing person's report, and a Detective Gurrola was assigned to Marshall's case. I obtained the two roommates' phone numbers from the deputy and immediately gave them a call. Both roommates stated to me that Marshall never said anything about leaving. Travis did tell me that when he was leaving to go to report at med hold, Marshall was still sitting at the table and appeared to be in no hurry to go to report himself. He stated, "Marshall was still sitting there when I left." That was the last time his roommates saw him.

I drove to the airport on Christmas Day, praying that Marshall would be there as scheduled and as promised. I rationalized that perhaps he'd just lost his cell phone, and that was the reason for the lack of communication. I sat there in my cheeriest Christmas sweater, with candy canes all over it, anxiously waiting to greet my son. I wore a smile and willed him to be there. I ached to hug him. Hope turned to despair when I realized the last of the passengers were trickling off the plane, and there was still no sign of him. Marshall would have been one of the first, I knew, and eager at that.

I went up to the ticket counter to inquire if my son was listed as a passenger on that flight. At first the agent was unwilling to give me that information. We locked eyes, and he could see how desperately worried I was. I was also doing my best to blink back the tears that were now starting to escape my eyes. He looked down, and with audible regret, confirmed that Marshall was not listed as a passenger on board that flight. I whispered "thank you," and as I walked away, I called Marshall's roommate Travis in San Diego. He said Marshall talked about how much he was looking forward to coming home for Christmas. He said Marshall was very responsible and intelligent. He said, "Your son spends money wisely and doesn't drink alcohol." He said Marshall accepted the inevitability of his discharge from the navy and was okay with it. Both roommates were genuinely baffled by his disappearance.

I headed home from the airport to a house full of visiting family members, all eagerly awaiting his arrival. Not wishing to spoil the festive Christmas mood, when I arrived home, I made the excuse that Marshall was unable to get away after all. "He was too busy," I said, "and the navy wouldn't let him leave. It's unfortunate, but these things happen." There were eight family members waiting in the kitchen to greet Marshall, and before I lost my composure, I made an excuse about freshening up and practically ran to my bathroom. There, I closed the door and sank to the floor. I sobbed with the knowledge that my son was as sick as they said he was.

DESERTER

In my quest to find my son, I was put in touch with a Lieutenant Healy on December 27, and learned that my new point of contact was a Commander Carl Klotzsche. Commander Klotzsche contacted me, and I gave him Detective Gurrola's name. The two of them spoke and agreed to work cooperatively to find Marshall. In the meantime, an HM2 (hospital corpsman second class) from med hold called and advised me that she had contacted the navy's legal department. She went on to say that if Marshall didn't turn up in the next thirty days, he would be considered a deserter. I was told that Master Chief Olsen from Marshall's previous command EODMU-3 (explosive ordinance disposal mobile unit three), O. was also notified of his disappearance.

    Marshall's roommates told me that all of his belongings including his laptop computer, clothes, contact lenses, and medication were still there in the apartment. They surmised that he wouldn't leave these things behind if his intent was to run away. Something else was worrying me. He had been trying to sell his motorcycle and parts from two storage units, having advertised them on Craigslist. His valuables included a rare 1960 Triumph. I pictured a scenario whereby he takes a prospective buyer to his storage unit and that person or people decide to knock Marshall over the head to simply steal the bike instead. I envisioned him lying there hurt, bleeding, with hands tied behind his back, and possibly locked up in his own storage unit. My heart raced with that mental picture.

    My fears and frustrations compelled me to write to

Illinois' fourteenth district Congressman/Speaker of the House Dennis Hastert. Marshall, having lived in and enlisted from Illinois, was a constituent, and I had to kick this into high gear. My greatest fear was that Marshall had met with foul play. My concern intensified with each day, and I pleaded with Hastert's office that they use considerable influence to elevate the visibility of my plight. After all, I reasoned, my son was an American serving his country:

This set into motion a whole series of events. I scanned photos of Marshall and forwarded them to Detective Gurrola. I was assigned a congressional liaison. A man named Dave Shelley with NCIS was going to investigate. I contacted veteran's affairs to request all Marshall's mail to be forwarded to me. I checked with the armed forces bank to see if there was any bank/ATM activity. Supervisor Jackie R. said they wouldn't comply without a court order. On January 17, 2006, Dennis Hastert's office called and offered to forward a letter they received from the navy regarding Marshall. His office expressed concern about Marshall's disappearance. I got a call from NCIS Curt Thomas (supervisor crime squad). I had high hopes that now we were getting somewhere.

Past due statements started to arrive—Marshall's T-Mobile account was in arrears. An operator told me that Marshall's last three calls were made on December 14, 2005 to:

- Oceanside, California (navy related)
- Linda Vistad, California (navy legal department/med discharge related)
- El Cajon, California (navy attorneys, counseling)

I reported the phone as lost/stolen. I wrote a letter to the legal department of T-Mobile, explaining that Marshall was missing so no new charges would be incurred. With the letter, I attached a missing person's photo of Marshall along with police information.

I called Detective Gurrola and gave him this information. He made calls to those last three numbers that Marshall dialed. Gurrola was told that Marshall had an appointment with the navy legal department on December 14th but never showed up.

Detective Gurrola called to inform me that he was turning over the investigation to Sandy Curry with the San Diego Homicide Detail and that she would be calling me shortly. I kept imagining Marshall, hurt and unconscious, locked in one of his storage units. I knew I had to hurry. I logged onto Yellowpages.com and began to call every storage facility in and around the San Diego area. I did a ten-mile radius search from the naval base for storage sites. Every time I came up dry, and it was costing valuable time. Now I was convinced that Marshall lay bleeding and dehydrated on the floor of one of his units. On January 18, 2006, and on my fifty-first call, I spoke with someone named Michelle at Store Safe Miramar. She could hear the desperation in my voice and was sympathetic to my predicament. She offered to make some calls for me to other storage companies. She called me back and enthusiastically announced that she'd located Marshall's storage. The owner of Lock & Leave was only too happy to hear from someone, since Marshall was in arrears in payment for the two units he'd rented. I paid the past due amount and convinced the owner to open Marshall's storage compartments. To my great relief, Marshall was not in either of his units. I was relieved by this but still very troubled. *What happened to my son? How can someone just disappear?* This became an obsession. The moment I dropped James off at school or piano lessons or Tae Kwon Do, I got to work looking for Marshall all the while trying to maintain normalcy at home so as not to cause alarm. During this turmoil, life with our younger son, James, included a Pinewood Derby, a school field trip to the St. Louis City Museum, children's choir, swim lessons, and the Blue and Gold Banquet. I was leading a double life. James was not told that his brother was missing, and neither were the girls who were away at college.

Sandy Curry called a day or two later asking if I had dental X-rays for Marshall. This would help in identifying a body. Now they were talking about a body—not good at all. I mailed X-rays to her that very day, January 26, 2006. I also contacted border patrol almost daily in case he crossed the border into Mexico. I told Ms. Curry that I tried to get information from the armed forces bank, but they couldn't help me without a court order. She told me that she would contact the bank directly.

On the thirty-first of January, a nationwide missing person special bulletin was posted for all law enforcement agencies. I looked up the bulletin and sure enough, there was a picture of my son with his personal data, occupation (US Navy), vehicle (1975 Red Ford Pick Up), and last-known whereabouts (Marshall was last seen leaving his home in Bonita, California on December 17, 2005. Marshall is a car show enthusiast and enjoys motorcycles). I thought, *Surely he'll be found now that his picture is posted on the national website.*

I spoke with Sandy Curry daily, always anticipating that one day soon he'd turn up somewhere.

On February 1, Ms. Curry faxed me, "As Marshall's next of kin," requesting my signature for "Consent to confiscate and examine" Marshall's computer.

And then it happened. Later that same day, February 1, 2006, Ms. Curry informed me that there was ATM activity on Marshall's account in Yuma, Arizona, of all places! I rejoiced in knowing Marshall was alive but greatly distressed that he had run away from the navy before his discharge was finalized. I was also confused. *How could he knowingly worry his family this way?* Now I feared for the consequences for Marshall's actions.

And then, on February 16, I received a letter from the Department of the Navy:

> *This is to inform you that Fink, Marshall Robert has been officially declared a deserter from the United States Navy. Desertion from the armed forces is a felony and is a very serious military offense punishable under the laws and regulations governing the Department of Defense. When a sailor is officially declared a deserter (absent for more than thirty days) pertinent information is entered into the National Crime Information Center computer and forwarded to all law enforcement agencies to assist in the deserter's apprehension and detainment. Should the deserter be stopped for something as minor as a traffic violation, they will be arrested and placed in jail under a felony warrant and will remain incarcerated until physically turned over to the military authorities. It is in the best interest to return to military authorities without civilian law enforcement involvement. Often the sailor wants to return and do the right thing but is scared or unsure and needs encouragement. I sincerely feel we should try everything in our power*

to assist them in returning to military authorities. The only other alternative is having the sailor apprehended, since the seriousness of this offense increases with the length of desertion. I am soliciting your support in resolving this matter. Should you have any questions or information that might be beneficial, I urge you to contact the Navy Absentee Collection and Information Center.
Sincerely,
Francisco T. Garcia

This letter sickened me. I immediately called the NACIC, Navy Absentee Collection and Information Center, providing them the homicide detective's name and all the information I had up to that date. I informed them of the bank activity in Yuma. They asked if I knew exactly where Marshall was so they could send a team to collect him. I said if I knew exactly where, I'd go there myself!

The heartache was insurmountable, and I knew we faced a long road ahead. It was our hope at that point that the navy would provide legal defense on Marshall's behalf and due to his diagnosis of bipolar, they'd go easy on him.

My next thought was to contact the sheriff's department in Yuma, Arizona. I called the Yuma PD and spoke with Investigator Thomas, briefing him regarding the fugitive warrant out on my son. He said, "Marshall probably just wants to disconnect from the family and his roots, kind of do his own thing." He promised to call if he heard anything more. On February 26, I again called Yuma PD, and this time I spoke with Sargent George Mitchell. He was very helpful, and when I told him the location of the ATM, he stated to me that he lived close to that very ATM. He then volunteered to go take a look in the area for Marshall's older model, red, Ford truck. I did not want to get my hopes up, so I was shocked to hear back from him later that same day, telling me he did locate and speak to Marshall. He said Marshall's truck was parked at a motel, and he went up and knocked on the motel door. He said Marshall answered the door, was polite, and was in fact feeling guilty for worrying everyone. He was bored hiding out, with nothing to do but watch television all day, and readily went with Sargent Mitchell back to the detention facility. This was glorious news. It sounded so like Marshall to feel guilty for worrying everyone. I had high expectations that the navy would look at his case from the human aspect. I knew they had protocol, but he had an unblemished track record prior to becoming stricken with his disorder. I hoped we'd be given a chance to emphasize his performance before the change in his behavior. He was at the top of his class, and he was so very proud to be in the navy. It gave him purpose and focus.

Two letters of praise, prior to Marshall's illness:

Dear Ms. Gentles: 2 July 02

Fireman Marshall R. Fink has earned distinction as a Distinguished Military Graduate upon completion of Engineman School Class A Course at Service School Command, Great Lakes, Illinois.

Your son has received this special recognition because of his leadership abilities, outstanding military bearing, and academic excellence. His dedication and devotion to the naval service are far above that of his fellow students. Students who achieve this status are awarded a special certificate in recognition of their academic and military excellence.

The military decorum and academic achievement that your son has demonstrated throughout his assignment at Service School Command, Great Lakes, will be invaluable in the performance of his duties as a member of the United States Navy. You have my highest esteem for the support and encouragement you have given your son.
Sincerely,
D. A. Block
Captain, U.S. Navy
Commanding Officer

From: Commanding, USS *PELELIU* 1 May 03
To: EN2 Marshall R. Fink
Subj: Letter of Appreciation

Please accept my sincere appreciation for your outstanding performance of duties as Auxiliaries Division, Engine Shop Maintenance Technician from February 2003 to May 2003. Your exemplary and professional performance of your duties was critical to the completion of the ship's Tailored Ship Training Availability, Final Evaluation Period, CART II, and Underway Demonstration. Your performance during these major evolutions highlighted your abilities as a top performer. You are personally responsible for the outstanding material readiness condition of both Ship's Service Emergency Diesel Generators, four Reverse Osmosis Units, two Small Boats, and the ship's deck winches. Your preparation and maintenance of your spaces and equipment allowed several multifaceted duties to be completed expeditiously with outstanding results.

Additionally, you corrected numerous safety discrepancies, which would have been detrimental to personnel if left uncorrected. Your dedication to duty and superior performance reflected great credit upon yourself and the United States Naval Service!

Congratulations on a job well done.
Dennis D. Dubard

He also received this award:

"Honor Graduate" awarded to Marshall Fink for achieving a Final GPA of 98.13 percent at Engineering Common Core Course CIN A-651-0118 25 April 2002

MIRAMAR BRIG

I immediately contacted Commander Klotzsche, Sandy Curry, and Marshall's roommate Travis. The commander said Marshall would be processed by a disciplinary team. He said to give them a couple days to work on this, and if I didn't hear from Marshall by Friday March 3, 2006, I could call him back. Then, on March 3, Commander Klotzsche called to say Marshall would be picked up by navy personnel that next Monday.

On Monday March 6, the navy picked up Marshall at 4:30 p.m. to take him back to the naval consolidated brig (military prison) in Miramar, San Diego.

Then, on March 8, I received the following e-mail from CDR Klotzsche:

> Mrs. Gentles,
> Sorry I missed your call this morning. I got the message and thought I'd update you via e-mail so I could provide the below link.
> I did not see your son when he arrived in San Diego late Monday night. Upon arrival, he was escorted to the naval consolidated brig, Miramar, California, where he is in pretrial confinement in order to ensure his staying around for legal processing.
> I am not at liberty to discuss the specifics of his case, but I can assure you that he will be well taken care of and will receive all the legal rights afforded him under the Uniform Code of Military Justice.

He then gave me my new points of contact for legal matters; ABEC Tracy Adler and LNC Don Osborne. They had also received copies of Klotzsche's letter to me.

Although I had asked, I was not allowed to speak with Marshall during his stay at Miramar.

I called the legal department on several occasions and was told that Marshall was not assigned legal counsel yet. I was told to keep checking back every couple of days. This was a frustration. I worried about what jail time does to the troubled mind and hoped he was being engaged in conversation with someone.

Finally, I was informed that a Chief Osborne, whose position, as explained to me, is a type of middleman between the prosecution and defense, and a Lieutenant Commander Messer could help me with a timeline so I could better understand what comes next.

On the thirtieth of March, I was informed that Marshall had been assigned to legal counsel, Lieutenant Connel.

I wrote the following letter and emailed it to Lieutenant Messer with copies distributed to Lieutenant Connel, Chief Osborne, and Commander Klotzsche on April 3, 2006:

> *Dear Lieutenant Commander Messer, 04/03/06*
> *I am writing on behalf of my son EM2 Marshall R. Fink who is currently being detained at the Miramar Brig.*
> *Prior to this recent incident, Marshall's record was unblemished and beyond reproach, having served four years without incident. Marshall flourished in the navy and was steadily moving up in the ranks with the intent to reenlist and make it a career. All of that changed suddenly last summer*

2005 when he started to exhibit unusual behavior resulting in his hospitalization in September 2005 at the Naval Medical Center. He was diagnosed with bipolar disorder. Marshall challenged the diagnosis but subsequently relented and complied with the prescribed medications. He became distraught to learn he was to be medically discharged and attempted to challenge that decision. He stated to me and his commanding officers that he felt capable of and confident that he could continue with his assigned duty. Marshall became discouraged and downtrodden, however, when he was informed that he could not change the situation in spite of his proactive efforts. It was too late, and his fate had already been determined. He was transferred to TPU where he awaited discharge proceedings set to become finalized in January 2006. In our phone conversations, he expressed enthusiasm about coming home for Christmas. When he didn't arrive at the airport on Christmas Day as scheduled we became concerned and alarmed. At that time Marshall disappeared, and all communication ceased. He was eventually apprehended in Yuma, Arizona, on February 28, 2006 and was returned to the naval command in San Diego on March 6. Marshall was assigned legal counsel, Lieutenant Connell on March 30th and is presently awaiting trial.
I am asking that the tribunal take Marshall's prior exemplary record into consideration when determining his fate.

> It is my conclusion that the psychological turmoil Marshall endured, as a result of the realization that the military no longer required his services, frightened him and impaired his judgment.
>
> I would appreciate correspondence from your office outlining an approximate time frame for Marshall's trial and judgments.
>
> I would like to add that this once exceedingly communicative, thoughtful, proud, and positive son of mine has not contacted anyone since December 11, 2005, which is highly uncharacteristic of him. This leads me to believe that he is embarrassed and ashamed of his dismissal by the military.
>
> It is my sincere desire and I implore you to grant leniency toward Marshall under the circumstances and allow him to retain full medical benefits through the VA system. It is evident that he will need medication for an undetermined if not indefinite time.
>
> Thank you for your consideration.
>
> Sincerely,
>
> Shirlee Gentles

The next day, I received the following e-mail from Commander Klotzsche:

> Mrs. Gentles, I authorized your son's release from the brig effective yesterday. He will be separated from the navy within the next ten days. In the meantime, he will be at TPU.
>
> Regards,
>
> CDR Carl Klotzsche, USN
>
> C.O. TPUSD

The same day that Marshall's separation from the Navy became official, I started to experience chest pain and heart palpitations. I lost my father to a myocardial infarction at age fifty-two and two of my three siblings also had M.I.'s at age fifty-one, my exact age. I was a little concerned so as a precaution, called to schedule an appointment with a cardiologist.

I wrote back to Commander Klotzsche:

Commander Klotzsche, 04/05/06
Thank you so much for authorizing Marshall's release. You have kept me informed about procedure and protocol, making it possible to cope during this emotional ordeal. Is Marshall's discharge honorable, dishonorable, or perhaps medical? Will he retain his benefits even though he may not think he needs them? When exactly will he become officially separated so that I can make travel arrangements to go see him?
Sincerely,
Shirlee Gentles

On the same day, I received a response:

Greetings Ma'am,
Sorry I wasn't able to take your call yesterday afternoon. Things have been extra busy this week, and my XO is on leave. As for your questions, Marshall has a normal work day routine at this point and is staying in our TPU discipline barracks while his administrative separation paperwork is being finalized. I'm being told his last day in the navy should be 11 April.
Marshall should be the one to discuss his discharge and benefits status with you. If you want to reach him or get a message to him, you may call.

> *I wish you the best in working things out with your son.*
> *Regards,*
> *CDR Carl "Klutch" Klotzsche*
> *Commanding Officer*
> *NRSW Transient Personnel Unit/co_TPUSD@navy.mil*

I said a silent prayer asking for leniency and hoping with all my might that Marshall's discharge would be deemed honorable. I prayed for a positive outcome and also for some closure to this incredibly painful ordeal.

Marshall called me the next day, April 6. He was remorseful, apologetic for worrying us, and there was a real sadness in his voice. He told me he had to sign the discharge papers, which read "Other Than Honorable." He sounded defeated. I told him everything would be fine. The important thing was that he was okay. I asked him to please come home where he could relax and in time make plans for the next phase of his life, which I hoped would be college. I told him we'd get through it and look ahead toward the future and put the past behind us. He said "Mom, I didn't mean to run, but I didn't hear any positive feedback from the navy. I don't have this bipolar illness." He pleaded, "Can we work on seeing if they'll change their minds and take me back?" He desperately wanted to remain in the navy, and this broke my heart.

Always the optimist, I knew that if I could convince Marshall to come home he could have a fresh start and make plans for a new career path. He could get back on his feet and even go back to school. Marshall told me that he appreciated my offer, but he wanted to try and make it on his own. He wanted to get an apartment with some friends and look for work. I admired his sense of responsibility. I told him the offer had no expiration. I told him I'd talked to his dad and Dick missed him and wanted to see him as much as I did. It had been a stressful ordeal for the entire family. I think we all just wanted to give Marshall a hug, really. He promised to keep in close contact with us and said he'd like to fly home for his birthday, which was the best news a mom could hear.

MARSHALL'S VISIT

On May 6, 2006 I had a stress test ordered by the cardiologist and the results were normal. It appeared as though all was fine, but I was not sleeping well at night. I would wake up in a panic, with shortness of breath, rapid heart rate, shakiness and I had this maddening ringing in my ears. I would go into the kitchen so as not to disturb John, and lean against the kitchen counter until I felt sleepy again.

On the sixth of July, I flew out of bed; the room was spinning. I sat on the floor feeling nauseated and shaky, trying my best to breathe slowly, while fighting the urge to throw up. This happened again the next night and I scheduled an appointment with my primary physician.

Each night started off fine. I'd fall asleep all right then wake in a panic, sweating, shaking, dizzy, feeling pressure in my ears, and heart racing. I could not catch my breath. I attributed the dizziness to a spinning ride I went on at Six Flags a few days earlier. My doctor asked me if I was under any stress. I gave him a brief overview of searching for Marshall, but when he offered me Prozac I was taken aback. I stated, "I don't need an antidepressant. I'm not depressed." He ordered an MRI on which he wrote, "MS (multiple sclerosis) concern." He gave me a prescription for Ativan, an anti-anxiety and insomnia medication, and the name of a psychiatrist, Dr. Mattingly. I didn't appreciate the suggestion of Prozac, but agreed it probably couldn't hurt to talk with someone about my concern over my son.

Later that month the results of my MRI came back and were negative for MS. It was normal scan, and all blood work and labs were also normal. I was diagnosed with "inner ear disturbance" and referred to an audiologist for an ENG (balance) test.

I awoke every night with dizziness and severe, pulsating pressure in my head which radiated to my extremities. I kept a writing pad next to my bed and on July 31, I jolted out of bed and wrote in a shaky hand: "Intense brain activity, brain rapid-firing, pressure, head pulsates, every muscle in my body quivers, especially my legs. I went into the kitchen and took an Ativan. I decided that I must see a neurologist. On August 2, a mutual friend of ours called to talk to John. When he asked how I was doing, I surprised myself by being rather candid. I told him that I hadn't been sleeping well and had a sort of brain tremor. He stated matter-of-factly, "You must see my doctor, Dr. JB." Desperate for relief from the maddening symptoms, I called the neurologist that day.

His office was located on the eighteenth floor of the hospital. I took a copy of my MRI with me and asked him to look it over for a second opinion. He prescribed Lexapro and told me to take Ativan as needed. I didn't see how this could help with my symptoms, but he stated that it was for anxiety and depression. Even though I was convinced that my problem was physiological not psychological, I relented and decided to give it a try. Dr. JB's findings on the MRI read:

- Bio chemical change
- Nocturnal jerks
- Anxiety d/t stress, depression
- No inner-ear disturbance
- Brain 100% normal

He told me he sees three to four people like me daily which was a huge relief.

On August 4, 2006, Marshall flew in from San Diego

for a visit. We hadn't seen him since his diagnosis of bipolar disorder. It was so great to see him. Marshall looked healthy and fit. He spent time with his little brother James. I didn't ask him about his medications. It was evident that whatever he was doing was working.

I developed an allergic reaction to the Lexapro the next day and the doctor switched my anxiety meds to Zoloft. On August 8, my bedside notes read, "Nocturnal jerks, increased heart rate, insomnia." As if to confirm this, John told me that my body jerked less than one minute apart for the entire night!

When I got together with my girlfriend Terri later that day, I was very anxious and restless. I simply could not relax and have a good time with my best friend. *What was happening to me?*

On the eleventh, we celebrated Marshall's twenty-fifth birthday. All four kids were in town, and it was a much needed and fun reunion.

In an effort to be proactive, I began taking meditation classes the next day to help me cope with my increasing anxiety. We were all given a breathe rock, which I started to carry in my pocket.

A friend of mine, who is a professional photographer, took family pictures of all six of us at our local exercise facility, the RecPlex. I felt better than I had in a couple of months, and it was a joyous day. Everyone was relaxed and enjoyed the photo shoot, which was evident by the resulting pictures. Marshall clowned around, posing with his hand on his hip and wearing sunglasses, always so attentive toward his brother. All four kids had a lot of fun. During his stay, Marshall saw a couple of his friends and played with James. John cleaned his teeth (my husband is a dentist), and we enjoyed catching up.

As I was driving Marshall to visit a friend a couple days after his birthday, I became very anxious in the car. I tried not to show it, but it felt like the walls were closing in on me, and I became nauseated. After dropping Marshall off, I called the doctor and they offered to see me right away. When the door started to close on the hospital elevator, I felt a rush of panic. I said, "Wait a minute, I forgot something," and stepped off. I then proceeded to walk up the eighteen floors to his office.

Dr. J.B. told me to decrease my Ativan, but stay on the Zoloft with a possible increase of Zoloft in a few weeks. I went to bed that night and awoke at five thirty in the morning with tremors. My teeth were chattering, my body was jerking, and my facial muscles were twitching out of control.

On August 17, 2006, my girlfriend Terri and her daughters Jaclyn and Rachel stopped over to see Marshall. Marshall was talkative, entertaining, and funny. We talked about what a hassle it had become to fly on an airplane since 9/11, what with the time-consuming check-in and security. At one point, to everyone's surprise, he pulled out a switchblade and out popped an enormous blade. Although his personality was shining through, there was something a little frightening about his demeanor. The four of us girls noticed this and made eye contact a few times, but then I dismissed it.

    Marshall left to go back to San Diego on August 19. We told him he was welcome to move back home anytime. I told him he could look for work, visit with his dad since he was only a five hour drive away, and go back to school if he wished. He said he would think about it and let us know.

ANXIETY/PANIC

I called Marshall on September 5th to check on him. He sounded anxious, breathless. He told me of the living conditions at his apartment complex in San Diego. He and his roommates had to chase a rat out of their unit. He said the rat had chewed out the entire underside of their couch. Then he said, "There are ants everywhere." I calmly asked what he meant by "everywhere." He said they crawled all over the kitchen counter, all over his protein powder and vitamin bottles. He told me that he had to keep all the caps screwed on tightly or the ants would get in. As I tried to sound calm, this mental picture he was painting made me panic. I asked if he could get the landlord to spray for bugs. He laughed at that. "It's not that kind of place, Mom. They don't care. It's low rent." These conditions were deplorable, and I was desperate to get him to come home.

I said, "Marshall, please come home. You will have a clean, bug-free room!" I tried desperately to remain calm, but my heart was racing. All my emotions were way out of control, way out of proportion. Marshall told me that he did in fact rent a U-Haul just in case, and he would let me know if he decided to come home. This was the most fantastic news I'd ever heard. Getting a U-Haul meant that he was serious. I knew it would be good for both of us if he came home. We could both heal.

On Friday September 8, 2006, John and I had planned to go out for dinner with our good friend Hugh and his new friend Judy. Marshall called me that morning, and it was hard for him to talk. He sounded so nervous, something I was not accustomed to hearing from Marshall.

He was extremely anxious. He told me that he decided not to move here after all. He said he wanted to make it on his own, be his own man. His voice was shaking and was thick with anxiety. He said that he would just have to lose the deposit on the U-Haul. In an instant I made the decision not to try and talk him out of it. I did not want to add to his obvious distress. I reassured him, encouraging him to do what he thought was the best. I said, "Marshall, please don't give it another thought. I admire you for wanting to be independent. I believe in you and know you can achieve whatever you set your mind to." He sounded relieved that I didn't try to talk him out of his decision. I told him that I loved him so much, was proud of him, and promised that we'd call him often.

It was after we hung up that I fell apart. John was at work, and James was at school. I was free to let all my emotions out. I cried and cried, so worried about what would become of Marshall. I knew he wasn't taking his medication. He couldn't afford it, and since his discharge was "other than honorable," the government wouldn't pay for it. It was just a matter of time before he became manic again. Who was going to help him when that happened? I thought again about his living conditions and became sick with worry. I called my sister Pat and unloaded on her. I told her that I decided to let Marshall go to set his own course. But deep down I knew he needed help, help that he couldn't get on his own. I reasoned that Marshall had no family or real friends in San Diego, and that he was living in a rat-and-ant-infested, low-income apartment and was too far away for me to help him. Plus, he had no tangible plan for the future. Pat and I talked and talked for well over an hour, while I paced from dining room to kitchen, wearing a long-worn path in the floor. I told Pat that I had no intention of going out that night with friends. I quite simply was in no shape to socialize. She said, "Shirlee, you must go. Don't stay at home and worry. You'll just make it worse." She said, "You must get out and spend time among friends." I would never have gone if not for her insistence and reluctantly took her advice.

I rode along with our friends, the Riley's, that evening because John was meeting us at the restaurant from work. I felt a little panicky in their car and told them briefly about my concerns for Marshall. At dinner I sat next to Hugh's friend Judy, and we hit it off right away. Hugh, in his intuitive way, could tell that I was struggling. He asked about Marshall. I told him through my tears, which I tried in vain to suppress, that Marshall had decided not to move back home. He was so sympathetic, knowing how important it was to me to have Marsh back at home. Then to my horror, while envisioning Marshall living in those deplorable conditions, I started to have a full-blown panic attack in the restaurant. I was hyperventilating and was terrified. I looked at Judy with what must have been wild eyes, and she immediately took charge of the situation. Perhaps it was the fact that she was a seasoned Yoga Practitioner, one who uses yoga to relieve stress and to find inner peace and balance. But whatever the reason, she read my fear and commanded, "Look at me, look into my eyes. Breathe. You're okay. Just take a slow, deep breath. Take it in slowly…now hold it…now let it out." I stared at her and followed her instructions to the letter. It was starting to work, and I relaxed, finally. She calmed me, she talked slowly, and she offered much encouragement, to my great relief. I started talking about Marshall, telling her about his bipolar disorder, his hospitalization at the Naval Medical Center, his discharge from the military, and about looking for Marshall for three months. She listened to me and offered: "Think of it this way, you are at the lowest place now, but it will slowly get better and better." She said, "There is only one way to go from here, and that's up." She said, "Look at it like this, your son wants to be a man. He'll be okay. Let him go. You must let him go." I promised to do just that. She was so helpful to me that night; I will always be indebted to her. We exchanged phone numbers and promised to keep in touch. She said, "Remember, it's all about the breathing," which I knew from my meditation and Yoga classes but needed to implement.

Over the next two days I weaned myself off of the Zoloft. I repeated to myself, "I will get better. Marshall will be fine. This too shall pass." I fell asleep that night for the very first time with no worries, sleeping soundly like I hadn't done in a very long time, until…

COMING HOME

On the fifth anniversary of the 9/11 tragedy, at two in the morning, the phone rang. I reached for the phone, and it was Marshall. "Oh, Marshall, this is a surprise. Is everything all right?"

He said, "I'm in the garage. Will you unlock the door?"

I was stunned and couldn't believe what I was hearing. *Didn't I just talk to Marshall yesterday, or was it two days ago? He was in San Diego two days ago. When did he change his mind about coming, and how did he get here so fast?* I was trying to mentally calculate how he could possibly have driven all that way in less than forty-eight hours. I sprang out of bed and ran to the garage door. I flung open the door, and it *was* Marshall. I was not dreaming. My excitement quickly turned to fear. His eyes were wild. I said, "Marshall, it's so good to see you." I reached out to hug him. He stood there, wooden, his eyes darting around the kitchen. I said, "Son, I'm so glad you decided to come home after all. What made you change your mind?" He didn't answer. Then I said, "C'mere, Marsh. Let me see you. Let me give you a hug." He walked right past me and over to the window blinds. He proceeded to systematically close every blind. I said, "Marsh, what are you doing? You must be tired after that long drive. Can I make you something to eat, or would you rather just hop into bed, and we'll talk in the morning?" Without saying a word, he walked back into the garage and started to close the two shades out there. I tried to hide my rising panic. "Marsh, what are you doing, son?"

His words were caustic, assaulting my senses. He said, matter-of-factly, "People can look in here. You've got an expensive car in the garage. You don't want anyone looking in at it."

I wanted the charade to end, but Marshall was not smiling. To my horror, Marshall grabbed the pitchfork hanging on the wall. I asked what he intended to do with that. He answered, "I'm just going to turn a little mulch." *God, help me.* That was when I knew with absolute certainty that the naval doctors' diagnosis of bipolar disorder was accurate. My worst nightmare could not compare to the real-life nightmare I was witnessing.

I followed Marshall as he walked out to the front yard. He stuck the pitchfork into the ground, and I blurted out, "Please, Marsh, don't worry about that now. We can do that another time." He stopped and then opened up the back of the U-Haul truck. He started to rummage around in the back of the truck, and I looked inside the cab area. I saw two empty cans of an energy drink and empty coffee cups.

I had cleared out one side of the garage when he first told me that he got the truck and thought he'd be coming home. It was still empty even after he told me he'd changed his mind. He carried a couple of boxes from the truck into the garage. Then he carried those same two boxes back outside and loaded them onto the truck. I thought he must be hyped up on caffeine and needed some food to help him sleep, but he ignored my suggestion for food. Instead, he reached for a ladder-like ramp and latched it onto the back of the truck. He went to untie a Yamaha motorcycle that was strapped against the far wall. While he wheeled the motorcycle down the ramp, it was evident that I would not be able to change Marshall's mind about going to bed. So I decided to help him, hoping he'd eventually tire out. We didn't stop until all his boxes were in the garage. His belongings filled the one side completely, even stacking some two to three boxes high. It must have taken us close to three hours, and both of us were sweating. I was exhausted, but Marshall was like a machine. I asked Marshall if he left San Diego immediately after we spoke on Saturday afternoon, and he didn't answer me. I thought, *This isn't humanly possible, unless, of course, he never stopped to sleep.*

I said, "Well, now that that's finished, how about heading to bed?" I said, "You probably missed your comfy bed. Let's go downstairs." We went down to his room in silence. I told him good night and then headed back upstairs.

It was now time to get James up for school, and John was just waking up, both having slept through the night undisturbed. John asked, "Was that Marshall you were talking to on the phone last night?"

I said, "Yes, but he's here. He decided to move back home, and he's really, really hyper."

John said, "He'll be all right after he gets some sleep."

I had an appointment that morning with Dr. J. B. I couldn't wait to tell him about Marshall so he could advise me on how to go about getting help for Marshall. Once again, I walked up the eighteen flights to his office, still claustrophobic from the lingering effects of the Zoloft. I was worried out of my mind by witnessing, first hand, Marshall's paranoia. I couldn't sit down and calmly relate what I'd witnessed. Instead, I paced back and forth in Dr. J.B.'s office while giving him the details of the early hour events. I asked again how I could go about getting help for Marshall. I had just witnessed my son in a full-blown manic/psychotic state of bipolar disorder, something I'd only read about before. And now I had just seen it in all its terrifying reality. I said, "My son didn't really come home at all. A stranger did."

Dr. J. B. looked visibly alarmed while listening to me describe Marshall's bizarre behavior. He said he needed to make a phone call. After the call, Dr. J. B. said, "The only thing I can recommend is to have Marshall picked up by the police."

I said, "I can't do that. He hasn't done anything wrong. How long will they hold him, and how will that help him? That's not the answer. There has to be a way to get him help, and I'm sure that's not the job of the police."

He said, "Well, I have no other suggestions." I thanked him but was disappointed with his advice. Marshall had come all this way. He came home, and I was going to do all I could to help him. I would find the resources. I was going to make it my mission to get real help for Marsh. I knew my determination and love would heal him—of this I was certain. And so began my quest, and I wasted no time. *Just breathe. You can do it!*

Marshall was in the garage, rummaging through his things when I returned. I ran downstairs to see if his bed looked slept in. It wasn't. I looked into his bathroom and saw the smashed remains of the fountain I was so fond of, the fountain that used to sit on the entry table for many years. I went back into the garage and asked Marshall what happened to it, he said, "I dropped it," but offered no apology.

I went back into the house and called the veteran's administration. I was told that there was nothing they could do since Marshall's discharge from the service was "Other than honorable." God, how I hated those words. I drove to the VA building downtown on Eighteenth Street anyway and filled out paperwork to apply for disability and health coverage for Marshall. I was told that in five to six weeks, Marshall would receive a VCAA (a disability pension benefit) letter. He would have to sign to start a claim, and they would need confirmation of his diagnosis. I thought, *I've got to start pressing forward to try every avenue I can to find Marshall some help.*

SELF-HELP

Still writing on my notepad every night in the dark, I tried to decipher the frenzied, scribbled mess in the morning. One morning my pad read: "Zoloft = panic attacks!"

I started to seek out self-help books, *Managing Your Mind* by Gillian Butler and Tony Hope, to gain insight for Marshall and books about hormonal imbalances in women. I used Yoga to help me cope with my stress. I concentrated on my breathing—long, slow breaths. The soothing and tranquil music allowed me to let down my guard. I could feel the tension escape. And by the end of each class and in the privacy of the darkened room, with my body in resting pose, my ears filled with my tears. I thought that if I healed myself, I would in turn, heal Marshall. This was the source of my stress.

Marshall had calmed down considerably. I always observed him closely, and he seemed to be doing better. At one point he walked upstairs carrying a roll of money in his hand. He said, "I want to give this money to John for letting me stay here." *Oh, so like Marshall*, I thought, *responsible and conscientious*. It made my heart melt when I heard John turn down the money. He reassured Marshall, "This is your house, too. You're welcome to stay as long as you like." This was an ice-breaker. At least I thought I witnessed Marshall start to relax. I'd hoped he'd begin to feel sufficiently comfortable to join us upstairs and become more sociable. I had high hopes—always the optimist.

More than once Marshall told me that he wanted the navy to take him back. I said, "Marshall, that's in the past. Once you are discharged, you have to move on and let it go." He told me that he thought about getting an attorney to prove that the military was wrong to discharge him.

He said, "Maybe I should get a brain scan and take that scan to the navy to prove that they were wrong about me. Because, Mom, that scan would show that I'm normal."

I offered encouragement. "Son, you're free to pursue other interests. How would you like to return to school?" But he looked forlorn. Nothing offered the fulfillment that he had in the navy. It was so hard to witness this. It just broke my heart.

I highlighted several passages from the *Managing Your Mind* book and gave it to Marshall. These included: "Understand the present"; "It is important to accept where you are now"; "The path that appears to wind wearily uphill may provide unexpected rewards later on." "Much of the future is not under our control"; Treat yourself right and learn to relax." He did pick up the book, and I hoped he'd gain some insight from it.

We were very active in our church, and I confided to our beloved Pastor Schult all the turmoil in our lives that started with the phone call we received from the navy, informing us that Marshall was sick. It brought us great comfort to know that he prayed for our family, and it helped us to cope.

Marshall was consumed with thoughts of returning to the navy by October of 2006. He insisted to me that the navy made a big mistake with his diagnosis. He truly believed that once the navy realized their error, he would be reinstated. I could not convince him otherwise.

From that point on, the month of October turned into a nightmare.

ARE YOU FEEDING ME POISON?

One night, Marshall told me that he had parasites in his head. He said, "I downloaded some sites that sell stuff to take that get rid of parasites."

I found out about a twenty-four-hour hotline called BHR (behavioral health response) from Greg Worzel's wife Katie and called them seeking advice. I spoke with someone at the hotline who told me that they have licensed professionals who are trained to deal with families in crisis. They are also available if you just need to talk to someone. It's confidential, and they'll even send someone out to your house if it's an emergency. I put their phone number on my speed dial.

On October 8, 2006, Marshall asked me that infamous question, "Are you feeding me poison?" I knew he was spiraling out of control, and it terrified me. I felt a rush of panic as he persisted. "Well, are you? Huh? Huh?" I knew a fundamental trust had been broken, and he was suspicious and paranoid. He asked, "Are you having me followed? Is John having me followed?" He would leave the house at all hours, sometimes long after we'd all gone to bed. I never slept. I listened for his return so I could get an idea of where he'd been. Sometimes he'd come home with a Walmart bag that always contained nonsense items—a toy gun that shot plastic cats; miscellaneous trinkets; and T-shirts with the following writing: "The Beatings Will Continue Until Morale Improves," "Pirates For Hire Specializing In Mayhem & Madness," and "Hail To The

King (Army of Darkness TM)" which had a picture of a man holding a chainsaw in one hand and a double-barreled shotgun in the other while standing on skeletons. He'd go to Blockbuster and rent the same type of movie—horror flicks showing mad doctors experimenting on the brains of victims. His favorite movie was *Hellraiser II*, a confusing tale about a disreputable mental hospital, torture, puzzles, and hell, which he would watch often. I wondered how he acted when he went on the outings. I was certain that he must have appeared odd to whoever waited on him. Then he offered, "People look at me funny when I go out to stores." Uh oh, my suspicions were right on. He was drawing attention. Then he asked a little differently this time, "Is John paying someone to follow me?"

I tried to reassure Marsh by saying, "Of course not. Why would he?"

Marshall started closely examining every bottle of water to make sure they weren't tampered with. He only drank from sealed bottles, never tap water.

I started to sort through his boxes in the garage a little every day, most of which were in huge containers. Everything was old and musty. He had saved a couple of empty tubes of toothpaste, old rusty razor blades, corroded batteries, all of which should have been thrown away long ago. There were old and outdated containers of protein powder—the ones I had sent him—and bag after bag of loose change. Other than the car and motorcycle parts, nothing was worth saving. I threw out the rusty, broken trash and washed the clothes that were salvageable. I found books and all the letters I'd written him. It was evident that he saved everything. *Strange, I never thought he was a pack rat.* I wondered if it was a result of his illness or if perhaps it was just the nomad existence, living out of boxes.

One night after Marshall tore off down the street in my car, I once again went through his containers. There was an old torn and tattered carry-on piece of luggage that I threw out. Then I saw something that made me catch my breath. I found a gallon Ziploc bag filled to capacity with large red capsules. I looked closer, and each capsule had the writing: www.supercaps.com on them. I came inside and Googled the Supercaps. They were advertised as: "Supercaps, energy booster, stimulant, maximum acceleration/minimum slow down, legal substitute to *amphetamine*, greatly increases energy levels. Each cap contains 66 mg of caffeine."

I read:
> In response to accumulating evidence of adverse effects and deaths related to ephedra, the FDA banned the sale of ephedra-containing supplements, such as Supercaps, on April 12, 2004.

Why on earth would Marshall have these in his possession, I wondered. But there was another shocking discovery. I found two jars, each filled with a white powdery substance. The jars were marked: "Caffeine Powder, Pharmaceutical Grade." Again, I Googled caffeine powder and read: "Bulk caffeine powder is extracted from pure coffee plants—boosts energy. Become more alert and increase concentration. Promotes better endurance in physical activities."

This was not only alarming but I was quite honestly shocked that Marshall had these in with his belongings. My son was so health conscious. He used to work out every day and chart his progress when he lived at home. Years ago I had told Marshall the story about his uncle Mike's experience with too much caffeine.

Back in the 1970s and after Uncle Mike graduated from college, he was accepted into the Peace Corps. His flight was leaving from St. Louis, Missouri, where I still lived with our parents. Mike drove up to the Chicago area to visit with our sister Pat before leaving the country. After sleeping very little, the next night, on the eve of his flight, he started to make the five-hour-drive back down to St. Louis. He was getting very tired and pulled over to get a cup of coffee. After his second cup of coffee he was still dozing off, so he pulled into a gas station. There used to be a product on the market called No Doz, and Mike bought it, hoping he wouldn't fall asleep while driving. By the time he arrived at the house, he was jittery and nervous and had severe heart palpitations. He was incapable of relaxing or falling asleep and did not want to eat. He said he felt sick and miserable even the next day as he boarded his long flight to Africa. Mike stated that he didn't feel right for months afterward, and that the episode made him intolerant of caffeine, which recurs to this day. For that matter, all of us siblings are sensitive to caffeine.

Marshall used to always read nutrition labels. He worked out and drank a lot of water. He was disciplined and dedicated to physical fitness. So finding the caffeine powder and ephedra stimulants frightened me. *Why on earth would Marshall take something that would hype him up?* This was serious stuff, and he had a mountain of it! I quickly threw all of it into a trash bag with a drawstring and placed it into the large can in the garage. The trash was to be picked up the next day, and I hoped that was the end of it.

That night James had his friend Sean over to spend the night. While everyone slept, I heard Marshall out in the garage. I opened the door from the kitchen and saw Marshall frantically going through his boxes. I said, "Marshall, it's late, what are you doing out here?"

He said, "What did you do with my stuff?"

I said, "What stuff?"

He raised his voice, asking me, "Where's the suitcase that was sitting right here? What did you do with the box I had over here?" His voice was getting louder and louder, and he was in a frenzy.

I said, "I don't know what you're talking about, Marsh." Then he opened the waste can and grabbed the black trash bag I had thrown out earlier that day. He started ripping through the trash and dumping all the contents just beyond the garage door and onto the driveway. The jars of caffeine powder flew out onto the driveway, as did the Supercaps. He started spouting expletives, repeating the offensive words over and over. He was enraged.

I said, "Marshall, please don't talk like that."

He replied, "I knew I shouldn't have [expletive] moved back here. Don't touch my stuff!"

While he continued to rant on and on, I pleaded with him, "Marshall, stop please. The neighbors will hear you."

He said, "You lied to me. You [expletive] lied to me."

I tried apologizing to him. "Marsh, everything was out of date, and anyway, why would you take ephedra and caffeine powder?" I tried to explain that these stimulants can trigger erratic behavior, especially in someone who already is sensitive to it. But he was livid and in a state of rage. I stood in the doorway and pleaded with Marshall to keep it down. I said, "You'll wake everyone up." I positioned myself to block or intercept him in case he decided to physically take out his fury on one of us. I apologized and promised not to touch his stuff. He kept saying the f-word over and over while I continued to plead with him.

He said, "I'll throw your stuff out. How would you like that? You don't respect me." Then he said, "I'll just drive my car off a cliff!" His rage continued for a solid three hours. I could not appease him as he continued to spew obscenities.

Finally I said, "Marshall, you cannot talk to me that way anymore. I will not tolerate it. You cannot talk to me like this in my own home. You have to respect me also. No more swearing!"

Finally at 3:00 a.m., he got into my car and tore down the street. I placed everything back in the trash except for the pills and powder, which he kept with him. I paced and paced while waiting for him to return. I kept wondering where he could have gone and if he'd be thrown in jail for speeding. I was sitting at the kitchen counter when I heard him return. He walked into the house and saw me waiting up for him. He said, "Hi, Mom, want to play dominos?" He produced a bag from Walmart that contained a metal tin of dominos.

I said, "Sure." I was so relieved to see that the rage was gone.

He said, "Mom, how could you know that these things you threw out weren't important to me? What if I had money hidden in the liner of my suitcase?"

I said, "You're right, Marsh." Then we played dominos as if it's a perfectly natural thing to do into the wee hours of the morning. I heard John get up and knew that it was 7:00 a.m. John said good-bye, having no clue of the events that took place overnight.

On October 9, 2006 I went to my appointment with

Dr. Greg Mattingly. I had scheduled the appointment knowing he was booked for a few months and that I could cancel it if I so chose. Now I was glad that I kept it. I told him everything. He was genuinely interested in helping me with my son. I told Dr. Mattingly that I was worried to death about Marsh. I asked him if he would be willing to treat Marshall, and he said yes. He stated that if I could get him there, he would treat him. He told me about the Crider Mental Health Center. He said I could talk to them to discuss an "Involuntary Commitment" protocol. This is something that I knew would have to be done very soon. I felt a weight start to lift a little and really felt good after talking to Dr. Mattingly. He didn't brush me off or suggest I have Marshall arrested. What he did do was offer to help me. I knew that I had found the right doctor this time!

- - - - - - - - - - -

Marshall came walking upstairs wearing a Hawaiian shirt he took from John's closet. He had a flower behind his ear, and he told me that he was going to a Luau. I thought, *No one would believe my life right now.*

So far, I was keeping up with James's busy schedule, and I was still singing in the church choir every Sunday. I went to my Yoga and Pilates physical fitness classes but stayed vigilant at home, keeping one eye on Marsh.

MANIC/PSYCHOTIC

On Saturday, October 14, 2006, while Marshall was upstairs in the garage, I began to straighten his bedroom and make his bed. I lifted his pillow and was alarmed to see a black handgun underneath it. I heard him coming back downstairs and quickly covered it up again. My mind was reeling with questions—*Is that Marshall's gun? Does he own a gun? Did he get one of our guns from under the stairs? Why does he have the gun under his pillow in the first place?* I decided that at the very next chance I had I'd take it away and hide it. I told John that I thought it would be a good idea to put a lock on the door under our steps where we stored a few guns. Once in a while, we'd go to the shooting range at Busch Wildlife. Even though we stored the bullets separately and never kept a loaded gun in the house, I said we'd better add the lock. John agreed, picked up a lock, and the next day we had it installed.

On the fifteenth, I again looked under Marshall's pillow, and the gun was gone. I felt around in all of his dresser drawers but didn't find it. I looked in his closet, and still no gun. I started to walk upstairs, and Marshall was waiting for me. He said, "They made me in charge of the world. They're trying to kill me."

"Who?" I asked.

He said, "C'mon, Mom. We've been through this already. You know who!" Then he repeated, "They're trying to kill me."

Again I asked, "Who's trying to kill you, Marsh?"

He replied, "The Africans, Russians—everyone. C'mon, Mom, keep up!" Then he became very giddy.

At 9:00 p.m., I went down to Marshall's room to check on him. In the most bizarre behavior yet, he asked this about his ten-year-old brother James: "Is he going to give us programs and inhibitions?"

I said, "What are you talking about, Marshall. You are not making sense."

Then shivers ran down my spine when Marshall asked, "Is James a Nazi? I'll hold him down and give him a swastika tattoo!" That statement threw my senses into high alert, and I was extremely alarmed and concerned for James's safety.

I said, "Marshall, James is your little brother, and he loves you and looks up to you. Now c'mon, please don't talk like this."

I bolted out of his room and ran upstairs to tell John what Marshall said. I needed help this time. While I breathlessly told John about Marshall's threat, I could feel Marshall breathing down my neck. John was stunned and loudly said, "Marshall, Marshall, Marshall, what are you talking about?" It was clear to me that John was just as afraid of Marshall as I was. I had no choice now but to enlist John's help. Previously, I tried to monitor Marshall's behavior on my own, but things were moving too quickly. I was not prepared for this swift shift into psychosis.

Marshall became giddy, which was so inappropriate it terrified me. He went back downstairs, and John said, "This is not good. Something has to be done about him."

Then Marshall came back upstairs carrying his laptop computer. He sat next to John on the couch and giddily said, "Here, I want to show you something that is really cool!" Then he proceeded to show John a video of an actual killing, a snuff video.

John stopped him immediately. He said, "Marshall,

that's not right. I don't want to see that. You can't look at stuff like that!"

I looked at Marsh and said, "We want you to see Dr. Mattingly, son." He left and went back to his room. I was terrified of Marshall now and decided I needed a new approach to get through to him. I went into his bedroom, slumped down in his chair, and with complete honesty said, "Marshall, please, you are killing me. Please go to the doctor. We just want to help you. We're so concerned for you." In my heart, I did feel like I was dying a little each day.

He looked right at me and paused a moment before stating, "[Expletive] you." I walked out of his room and immediately called his father, Dick.

I needed Dick to help me with Marshall. I wanted him to take Marsh for a while. Get him away from James. I needed to devote full-time effort to seek help for him, and I didn't want any distractions. I had to shield James from any and all turmoil. I was not going to take no for an answer.

Dick was not very receptive to my suggestion of driving Marshall up to Dundee, Illinois. I thought that perhaps when Marshall saw his dad he'd snap out of this state he was in and be jolted back to reality. Dick didn't want to deal with Marshall either, but I insisted. I knew John was losing patience, too. He wanted Marshall's dad to take over some of the responsibility. Dick reluctantly agreed, and I presented the trip to Marshall as enthusiastically as I could.

I baked Dick's and Marshall's favorite cookies, and we headed up to Dundee—a five-hour drive. My mom came along with us so she could keep me company on the drive back. Marshall was withdrawn and very quiet on the trip.

When we greeted Dick, Marshall's mood never changed. Gone was the day when he'd greet his father with a huge smile and hug. To compensate for the awkward reunion, Dick proceeded to point out all the exterior improvements he'd made to his house and yard. I snapped a photo of Marshall and Dick before leaving, praying that he'd start to slip into a comfortable exchange with his dad. I thought surely Dick's easy manner and genuine love and affection for his son would soon bring him around. I thought perhaps Dick could check into getting some help for our son, too. The photo haunts me even today. Marshall looks so gaunt. He has a pained expression on his face, and it was evident that he was dropping a lot of weight.

Mom and I got back into the car and headed back to St. Charles. We were all the way to Highway 270 at the Glen Carbon, Illinois exit, almost home, when Dick called my cell phone. He urgently told me that I needed to turn around and drive back up to get Marshall. I was stunned. This was very bad. I was counting on spending some time alone with John and James—needed time alone. I tried to convince Dick to keep Marsh, at least for a few days. Dick said, "Marshall is sitting in the driveway waiting for you to come back." Dick also stated that the first words out of Marshall's mouth were confrontational. He said, "Marshall looked down at the floor by me and said, 'Do you want a piece of me?'" Dick continued, "Marshall is very anxious. He refuses food and will not make eye contact." Dick said that Marsh had placed $2000 cash on his kitchen counter and took the keys to his car. As he started to walk out the door, Marshall said, "I have to get out of here!" Dick grabbed the keys from Marsh and said, "Son, if you take my car, I'll have to call the police." Dick said that's when Marshall slumped down in the driveway to wait for my return.

What could I do but turn around and head back up. I asked Dick to meet me halfway in Bloomington. It was clear that Dick had already given up. Now Dick got to see firsthand just how severely sick his son was, and I knew he felt helpless to do anything for him.

I pulled up alongside Dick's car in Bloomington, and we rolled down our windows. Marshall got into the backseat of my car, and Dick apologized to me. He said, "You're stronger than me. You've always been the strong one." Dick looked remorseful, defeated really. He said, "I love you, son." Then he slowly drove off. I saw Marshall watch his dad drive away, and it looked like he wanted to say something. He remained silent. Mom and I tried to engage Marshall in conversation to no avail. It was a long, somber drive back to St. Louis, and I felt the weight of the world on my shoulders.

When John saw me enter the house with Marshall, he said, "What…I thought Marshall was going to stay with his dad for a while?" When I said that Dick couldn't handle him, John said, "Well you gave in too quickly. Dick should be willing to help out." Marshall went down to his room where he spent the remainder of the weekend.

Monday, October 23, 2006, was red, white, and blue day at James's school. I accompanied his class on a field trip to the Daniel Boone Home. When we got home, I checked on Marshall. When I entered his room to talk to him, he got up off the bed, went into his closet, and closed the door. I couldn't talk him into coming out. He came upstairs once during the evening to get a bottle of water and returned to his room. Since he moved back home, he had never joined us for dinner.

> *I rarely sleep now, ever vigilant, keeping one eye focused on our open bedroom doorway. We have two electric eye sensors spanning the stairway that make a faint click when someone interrupts the beam. I hear this several times a night and know Marshall is coming upstairs. My hearing has become acute. I am on high alert and quite literally can hear a pin drop. When I hear that click, I lay perfectly motionless, hardly breathing, and watch intently to see if Marshall is coming into our room, or even worse, heading toward James's room. I let out a sigh of relief and breathe again when I hear the click signaling his return downstairs. I often think of the old Marshall and the way he used to say with such ease, "I love my Momma."*

I wrote of this nightly vigil on my ever present notepad after Marshall came upstairs at 2:00 a.m. While John and James slept-I remained on high-alert every night. The tears flowed when I thought of my beautiful son. Always so affectionate, he used to say "I love my Momma" often, and with sweet sincerity.

I tried again to convince Marshall to go see Dr. Mattingly. It was October 29, 2006, and I told him that I loved him and wanted him to be a happy. I told him that the doctor could help him deal with his inner turmoil and stated, "We can see that you are struggling and know that you don't like to feel this way. Let the doctor help you overcome these hurdles." I said, "Let's just face our problems head-on, Marsh, and deal with it."

He answered with an emphatic "No, I won't talk to him. I'll just kill myself!"

The next day my brother Mike called, and I told him about Marshall's steady decline. I was anxious and breathless, pacing around John's office with the door closed, in case Marshall was listening. I spoke in a hushed, urgent tone as I relayed the events of the disastrous visit with his father. I repeated Marshall's words from the night before. Mike was so concerned for all of us, but mostly, he just sounded so sad.

On October 31, 2006, I wrote the following letter to the VA, asking for disability benefits for Marshall and pleading to change his discharge status to medical instead of "Other than honorable."

> *Veterans Service Center Manager, 10/31/06*
> *Events that lead to Marshall Fink's discharge: Marshall served in the navy from 1/17/02 until leaving active service on 4/11/06, without incident. His record was unblemished and exemplary. He thrived in the military and intended to make it a career. His service was honorable. (See attached letters of recognition for excellent service record).*

Marshall has always been a confident, motivated, cheerful, and optimistic person who makes friends easily. We were all so proud of his decision to join the navy following September 11, 2001. (See enclosed photos of a healthy, vibrant, well-adjusted Marshall). Without warning and to his superior officer's (Master Chief Markholtz EOD 3) surprise, Marshall started to exhibit unusual and uncharacteristic behavior and was admitted to the Naval Medical Center on September 22, 2005. Doctors there determined that his behavior was consistent with bipolar disorder. The doctors in charge of his care are listed on the enclosed medical forms. The last doctor to give him care was J. M., MD.

Managing bipolar disorder requires lifetime maintenance and compliance with medication. His discharge was to be a "Medical Separation." Marshall, as you can read in his handwritten notes while hospitalized, was greatly distressed to be dismissed from the military. He believed then and still contends now that the navy made a mistake about his diagnosis and will inevitably realize their error and reinstate him to active duty. He believes that he still has a lot to offer them.

Everything was happening too quickly for him. In his panic and turmoil at the realization that his services were no longer needed and compounded by his disorder, his judgment was impaired, and he went AWOL in a hopeless effort to delay the inevitable. His apprehension led to his "less than honorable" discharge instead of the previous "Medical Separation." Regardless, he was informed that he was entitled to receive disability and health benefits. He declined to furnish the necessary paperwork for these benefits, fearing that by doing so his medical/mental health diagnosis could become available and discourage future prospective employers.

He now resides with me, his mother, and stepfather in St. Charles, Missouri. His illness prevails and is quite evident, but he is unable to afford medical care. In his paranoia he asks if we are feeding him poison or having him followed—the list of unfounded accusations is endless. He's giddy one moment and withdrawn the next. He lacks confidence and self-esteem and will not make eye contact. He no longer socializes with anyone. The situation is sad and heartbreaking. He desperately needs help, but without benefits, we're at a loss to help him.

His decision to go AWOL was a derivative of his illness and definitely not premeditated. We do not know, at this time, if the service in the navy was the root cause of his sickness, but it absolutely manifested itself while he was on active duty. Marshall requires your assistance to have a chance to properly fight this disease. Please ensure that his discharge was indeed a "Medical Separation" and approve disability benefits for my son so that we can try to get him out of this awful situation and allow him to proceed with his life.

Thanks for your consideration.

Sincerely,
Shirlee Gentles

A few days later on November 3, 2006, I went down to Marshall's room and asked him how he was doing. He yelled, "Get out! Get the hell out of my room! You're mean." He was enraged, pursing his lips with a look of fury and hatred in his eyes.

I pleaded with him, "Marshall, look at me. Look into my eyes. Can't you see how much I love you and want only the best for you? Honey, let me help you."

He yelled back, "Get out of my way, or I'll snap you."

I said, "*Please*, Marshall, I'm your mom. I love you more than anything in the world." He walked right past me and went upstairs, grabbed my keys, and drove off.

I called Dr. Mattingly's office, and they advised to have Marshall picked up by the police.

I was pondering this when Marshall returned with the car. I called the Crider Center, and a counselor advised me to fill out paperwork to start a civil involuntary detention. I sent the following Fax to Dr. Mattingly's office.

> *Dr. Mattingly, 11/3/06*
>
> *As per your suggestion, I was going to have my son Marshall Fink picked up by the police, but he returned with my car. I called the Crider Center in Wentzville, and a counselor (Linda) advised me to fill out civil involuntary detention paperwork on Monday. Too late today. I'm to take that paperwork along with two sworn affidavits regarding Marshall's behavior to the St. Charles courthouse for approval by a judge. He can then be taken against his will to St. Joseph Hospital for ninety-six hours.*
>
> *I will contact your office once this is set in motion, and I can't thank you enough for helping me with my son.*

Sincerely,
Shirlee Gentles

Marshall stayed in his room all day on the fourth. I never saw him. I sang at both church services the next day. Afterward, I took James and a friend to the city museum downtown. When we returned, I never saw Marshall. He stayed in his room.

I had an appointment at the Crider Center on November 6 to obtain the necessary paperwork for the civil involuntary detention, giving permission to have Marshall taken to St. Joseph Hospital where he would be detained for ninety-six hours while being treated by Dr. Mattingly.

That evening, John and I had to compose statements that necessitated having Marshall removed from the home.

My statement read:

- He exhibits paranoid behavior and asks if I am feeding him poison. He asks if we are having him followed.
- He states, "They are trying to kill me."
- He only drinks from sealed bottles.
- His behavior is unstable and erratic. Threatened to take my car and drive it off a cliff.
- He states that he thinks his ten-year-old brother is a Nazi and will hold him down and give him a swastika tattoo.
- He was discharged from the navy due to bipolar disorder but insists they made a mistake and will have to take him back.
- He became enraged when I tried to talk to him about getting help. He stated, "Get out of my way, or I'll snap you…"

- He takes Ephedra capsules on a regular basis.

John's statement read:
- I have noticed Marshall completely withdraw from any interaction with anyone since returning home on September 11, 2006.
- He has stated there are people following him.
- He thinks his mother is trying to poison him.
- Most days he stays in his room except for a few minutes where he comes upstairs to the kitchen for food or drink that he prepares.

I called Dick that night to tell him that we were going to have to have Marshall involuntarily removed from the house so he could receive treatment. I was pacing around John's office downstairs as I spoke to him. Dick agreed with that decision and reiterated that I was the strong one and that he couldn't handle it. I told Dick that I'm not that strong, but I'd do whatever necessary to help our boy. I said, "But it's taking a toll on my health."

Dick said, "Thank John for me too, would you?"

I said, "Here, why don't you do that yourself. It would be nice if he heard it from you." I handed the phone to John. I heard John say into the phone, "Well, it's okay. No problem. I appreciate that."

So that was done. I paced, feeling my heart beating out of control. I knew that the stress hormone cortisol had to be pumping into my system at a steady rate but remained determined to fight for however long it took, providing my body could withstand the assault.

I prayed with extra conviction that night. It had become the norm to kneel in the privacy of my bathroom at night, my hands resting on the counter and clasped in prayer. John would invariably walk in on me as I knelt there, motionless. He'd say, "Oh, you're praying again." This had become a coping mechanism that allowed the stress to dissipate. I could feel my body relax and my heart rate slow way down. I awoke the same way each morning as if I'd fought in a battle. I was winded and could hardly catch my breath. I was shaky and had to rest both hands on the bathroom counter to support my weight. I was utterly exhausted as if I hadn't slept at all.

I had Bunko on Tuesday November 7, and took the Involuntary paperwork with me. My girlfriend, Mary Beth, who I was picking me up that night, was a notary. I caught a glimpse of Marshall late that evening as he was entering his bedroom. He'd stopped eating completely, and he was getting very thin. His pants were baggy.

The next day I took the notarized statements and submitted them to the State of Missouri Department of Mental Health.

On the ninth, after James's piano lesson, scout pack meeting, and Blue and Gold committee meeting, I wrote a letter to Greg, the music director at our church, informing him that I had to drop out of the Christmas program. I was candid as Greg is a good friend of mine.

I told Greg about my son's steady decline from his manic/giddy state that included racing thoughts and boundless energy to the exact opposite extreme. I said he was now in the depressed state and stayed in his dark room with no interaction with us. Even when I tried to talk to Marshall, he closed himself in his closet and wouldn't answer me. There is no television on in his room or music of any kind. He'd lost a great deal of weight, and his clothes were falling off of him. I went on to write that I was trying to get disability through the VA, but that process was taking much time. I said that as a last resort John and I had to start an involuntary confinement through probate court in St. Charles. We'd be notified on the day that deputies would be dispatched to our house to physically take Marshall to the hospital. He would be detained for ninety-six hours and assessed by a doctor who would then determine whether or not to extend the detention.

I said that it is heartbreaking to see my son so completely withdrawn, and I felt that I had no choice but to take this next step. Knowing Marshall would be handcuffed and removed was going to be difficult to witness, and I knew Marshall would feel betrayed. But Dr. Mattingly told us that the longer we waited, the greater was the chance of permanent brain damage, in which case I had no choice.

In times of stress, I always remembered my brother Mike's pep talk years earlier. Our families were vacationing together in Africa. He handed me the keys to a rental truck because he had to leave to attend to something. It was a stick-shift, which I hadn't driven in years. Then I noticed that the steering wheel was on the right and gear shift on the left. To make matters worse, the road I was about to embark on was hilly. I told him I wasn't comfortable and didn't think I could drive the truck. He matter-of-factly said, "You can do it. You're a Nyquist. You can do anything you set your mind to!" This was spoken with such conviction that I summoned the courage and did it. He had confidence in me, and I was able to follow through. Funny how some things stay with you for life.

On November 20, 2006, and just prior to Marshall's hospitalization, I was scrambling to get him medical coverage. I hadn't heard from the veteran's administration, so I called the Crider Center for advice. They suggested that I call the hospital directly. I spoke with someone in central intake at St. Joseph Hospital that same day. They are a full-pay hospital, and they suggested that we apply for Medicaid. I called family services (St. Charles Family Support) and a woman named Bobbie Royce mailed me a medical assistance application and disability questionnaire. She said I needed to include Marshall's birth certificate, a photo ID, and his social security number, along with statements from the Naval Medical Center. Ms. Royce said that if the VA benefits were approved in the meantime, Medicaid could still be used in conjunction with those benefits. I was filled with optimism after that phone call and filled out all the forms when I received them the next day. I attached Marshall's discharge papers along with notes from all the doctors who treated him at the naval hospital. I was surprised to receive a letter from the Department of Veteran's Affairs stating that they were working on the application for character of discharge decision. It went on to read: "The military has said your service was not honorable. Therefore, we have to make a decision about your service. As long as we decide that your service was not dishonorable, you will be eligible for VA benefits." Our paperwork had been turned in on September 26, 2006, but I knew these things took time.

My contact at the VA regional office in St. Louis was Richard Ivey, and we'd already spoken on several occasions. His title was homeless veteran's coordinator. Prior to meeting with him for the first time, all avenues I pursued with the VA were met with closed doors. I had often been told that since I was the mother there was nothing they could do; they had to speak with Marshall directly. Even though I reasoned that my son was incapable of communicating with anyone and had withdrawn completely, it made no difference to them, and they would not waiver. Countless times I heard these words; "Sorry, we can't help you." Richard Ivey was the exception. He offered encouragement and showed compassion. He told me that Marshall's review would be coming up soon. I put my trust in him, confident that he had Marshall's best interests at heart and knowing he would review all the documents thoroughly and objectively.

I went to the Social Security administration on December 6, and applied for disability and supplemental security income on Marshall's behalf. I was trying to get my son help from all angles, and I was navigating through a governmental system that was completely foreign to me. I knew it was a race against the clock.

That night as with all nights, I couldn't sleep. I wrote: "Do not dwell on negative thoughts. Show an attitude of gratitude. I can do all things through Christ who strengthens me." I fell asleep praying, waking a short while later in a panic.

John, James, Heather, and I drove to Columbia, Missouri, without Marshall, to attend Allison's graduation from The University of Missouri at Columbia on December 16. We later celebrated at a local restaurant. Everyone in our extended family inquired about Marshall, and I gave them updated information. I told them that with the exception of dropping out of choir, I was trying to maintain consistency at home.

On the ninteenth, I met with an attorney from our church, seeking power of attorney and legal guardianship over Marshall.

I received a call from a probate court division clerk named Debbie on December 20, 2006. She was with the department that serves court ordered warrants for the involuntary commitments. She told me I needed to come in and sign the final papers so the sheriff's deputies could come and pick up Marshall. This was the day I both anxiously awaited and dreaded. I got in my car and drove to the probate office, dropping the dogs off at the kennel on my way. The last thing I wanted was the dogs anxiously greeting the cops, warning Marshall beforehand. After signing the papers, I asked when he'd be picked up and was told it would be sometime that very day, but they could not give me a time.

I might as well have signed his death warrant. I was suddenly struck with the most profound sadness I'd ever felt in my life. I was so overcome with emotion that before I could exit their office I broke down. Tears ran down my cheeks and dripped onto my shirt. I paused before opening the door to wipe my face and compose myself. I walked out of the building and headed home to await the arrival of the police.

INVOLUNTARY CONFINEMENT

The first thing I did when I got home was call St. Joseph Hospital to inform them that Marshall would be taken there some time that day. Bonnie in behavioral meds, told me that Marshall should first be brought to the ER, or intake as she called it. Several hours passed with no sign of the police. I was nervous, and the wait was getting to me. I couldn't leave the house and had to cancel James's swimming class and piano lesson. At 7:00 p.m., I called the sheriff's department and was told that I would be notified when they were on the way. I had given them my cell number so the phone wouldn't ring at the house. So far Marshall hadn't come upstairs all day, and I prayed that he wasn't upstairs when they arrived to get him. I purposely left the garage door up so it wouldn't make a sound when they arrived. The wait was intolerable. I threw a quick dinner together, and John kept James preoccupied. I paced and looked out the kitchen window constantly. I heard Marshall walking up the stairs, and I pretended to clean off the table and straighten the chairs. I offered him some food. He didn't say a word or even look at me. He simply got a bottle of water out of the refrigerator and headed back downstairs. He looked gaunt, weak, and thin, his belt on the tightest notch to hold his pants on. He was wasting away, and I knew we were getting him to the hospital just in time to save his life. I breathed a sigh of relief that no one showed up when he was in the kitchen.

It was maddening now, and at 11:30 p.m. I called

the sheriff's department. I thought if they weren't coming today after all, I wasn't sure if I could do this another time. Again, I was told that they were very busy today and that no one was available yet to pick up my son. I said, "But I was told that you would come today, and today will be over in half an hour!" A woman told me to sit tight, and they'd still try to squeeze it in today. John and James had been in bed for hours now, and there I was pacing, watching, pacing.

At 12:15 a.m., my cell phone rang, and I jumped like I'd been shot. It was raining steadily now, and a police officer told me they were just pulling down my street and were killing their lights. At that exact moment, I was looking out the kitchen window. Sure enough, I watched as three patrol cars drove around the curve out front and saw each car turn out their lights. I thought my heart would stop. I ran to our bedroom and whispered to John that the police were here then ran back to the kitchen and out the garage door. Three officers were getting out of their cars as I met them in the driveway. It was raining pretty heavy, and I quickly introduced myself. One of them asked, "Where is your son? Is he armed?" I told them he was not armed. They asked how strong he was and if he could possibly grab a weapon such as a baseball bat. I said he was weak and would offer no resistance. I told them I would first knock on Marshall's bedroom door, bringing a key just in case he'd locked it. Then I told the police that I would immediately head for his closet because he always went there in recent weeks to avoid me. I begged them to be gentle. I said, "He's the love of my life. He's sick and needs help. Please don't hurt him."

When we entered the house, no one said a word. They motioned to me with their hands, and all three hugged the wall as we made our way toward the stairway by way of the darkened dining room. One of them had his gun drawn. I saw John come out of the bedroom and freeze when he saw the four of us slinking around the corner.

I gently knocked on Marshall's door and, taking no chances, swiftly inserted the key into his lock. The three officers were directly in back of me, just inches away. I opened his door and walked directly toward Marshall's closet, just as Marshall himself was taking a step in that direction. In an instant all three officers were in the room. Marshall saw them and froze. I said, "Marsh, we love you, son. We just want to get you well. You are not in trouble or getting arrested. We're just taking you to the hospital." He instinctively turned and put his hands behind his back and was swiftly handcuffed. I saw John in the doorway at that moment and pleaded, "Tell him, honey."

John reassured Marshall by saying, "That's right, Marshall. We just want to help you. You're not in any trouble." One police officer reached in Marshall's pockets and pulled out a wad of money, along with his driver's license and passport. He had all the money he owned on him. He was fully clothed, right down to his shoes, and standing there thinner than he'd ever been in his life.

I asked the officers to please take Marshall to the ER at St. Joseph Hospital. I said I would follow behind them in my car. I had my girlfriend Terri on speed dial, and she was just waiting for my call. Her house is only a couple miles away, and she got to my house in an instant. We both got into my car and proceeded to follow the patrol cars to the hospital.

In admittance, Marshall was handcuffed to one of the beds. After asking if they could do anything else, the officers turned and left. I briefly explained to the attendant in admittance that Marshall was bipolar. I said that after a lengthy manic phase, when he thought we were trying to poison him and he threatened to hold his brother down and give him a swastika tattoo, he was now in the depressed and withdrawn phase and had stopped eating. I said, "Dr. Mattingly knows of his condition and will treat him." Terri and I talked softly to Marshall, offering reassurance. I gently rubbed his arm. He did not respond or acknowledge us in any way. A young woman came into the room carrying a blood-draw kit. She didn't introduce herself, just got out an alcohol wipe, tourniquet, and syringe. When she inserted the needle into Marshall's right arm, he bucked up against the restraints while suddenly sucking in a large amount of air, quickly expanding his chest. It was as if he'd just come alive. His neck and arm muscles bulged as he tried to get up off the bed. The girl abruptly stopped what she was doing, noticing him for the first time. She jumped backward and looked terrified then quickly fled the room. Shortly thereafter, a new young woman entered, carrying the same kit. I introduced Terri and myself and asked her to please explain what she was about to do to my son directly. She was calm and talked to Marshall as she inserted the needle. He let her draw blood without resistance. Afterward, an ER doctor walked in, and in a rather threatening tone—at least I thought so anyway—said, "So, you tried to strangle your brother, heh?"

Marshall, who'd been looking straight ahead, suddenly turned to glance in my direction, and we made brief eye contact. He had a look of confusion on his face, his eyes momentarily questioning mine, as if I'd told this doctor a lie. I very calmly corrected the doctor by stating, "No, he was going to give his brother a tattoo." I wanted to tell him that he should get it right. His approach was threatening and accusatory, not at all how I expected a doctor to act. As they were preparing to take Marshall up to the behavioral med floor, I reinforced that Dr. Mattingly agreed to be his doctor since he was familiar with Marshall's medical history. I was told that we could leave now and that they'd have the doctor's office call me the next day.

I knew that Dr. Mattingly made rounds in the morning, but when I didn't receive a call by late afternoon, I called his office. They knew nothing about Marshall's admittance the night before. No one informed them from the ER, even though I had twice stated that Dr. Mattingly said he would treat my son. I was very alarmed and said, "Oh no, who *is* treating him?"

The nurse said, "No need to worry, we will get it straightened out." They called back in about ten minutes and told me that a psychiatrist by the name of William Wang had seen Marshall but knew nothing of his history. I was reassured that Marshall's care could be turned over to Dr. Mattingly, but I would have to speak directly to Dr. Wang to state my preference. I called and spoke to Dr. Wang, thanking him for treating Marshall. I said there must have been a miscommunication in the ER because Dr. Mattingly knew the details of Marshall's medical history since being diagnosed with bipolar disorder in the navy and offered to treat him.

In the meantime, my girlfriend Terri and her daughter stopped by the hospital to see Marshall. She was talking to me on her cell phone while peeking through the glass at Marshall. She told me he was pacing in the television area behind the nurses' station. When she got up the courage, she rang the bell next to the door. A nurse asked them to step inside the door because no one could leave. Marshall was called over to his guests. Terri gave Marsh a cheerful greeting. "Hi, Marsh, its Aunt Terri and Jaclyn." She wanted to hug him but resisted the urge because he didn't acknowledge her. She said, "You remember Jaclyn?" They had recently visited, and of course, Marshall had known her since he was a toddler. Terri said he looked through them and above them and kept his eyes on the door. They stayed only briefly before Terri told him that she loved him and was thinking of him.

Once the doctor mix-up was resolved and just before his care was turned over to Dr. Mattingly, I received a call from the psych floor that Marshall had assaulted Dr. Wang, pinning him to the floor. Security was called, and Marshall was pulled off the doctor and restrained. She stated that it took four guys to get Marshall restrained. I blurted out, "Dear God, did anyone get hurt?" She said no but he was put into a private room and assigned a twenty-four-hour suicide watch. She said that Dr. Wang was fine and declined medical treatment. I was quite certain that this Dr. Wang was only too happy to transfer Marshall's care to someone else.

I baked Marshall's favorite cookies and took them plus some clean clothes to the hospital. Once I was buzzed in, I stopped at the nurses' station so I could be directed to his room. There was someone sitting directly across from his door, watching him. It was reassuring to know that Marsh was in this safe environment and was receiving care. I walked in and scanned his body for telltale signs of struggle. I was relieved that I didn't see any bruises or scratches and was especially thankful that he didn't hurt the doctor. That may have caused problems for both of them, and I shuddered to think about that. I thought, *Perhaps Marshall was just confused and felt abandoned when Dr.*

Wang told him that he was turning over his care to a different doctor. I'll never know why he attacked the doctor because they said he spoke not a word since being admitted. I spoke softly to Marsh, telling him that I loved him. He turned away and looked very tired.

On Saturday, I again visited Marshall after making John and James some dinner. His nurse told me that he refused to talk today. I rested my hand on his arm and told him that I loved him so very much. It was hard to see him like this. It was much like home—quiet, dark room with no communication.

On Christmas Eve 2006, Heather, Allison, and I went to the hospital. The girls tried to talk to Marshall, but he didn't say anything to any of us. It was hard for the girls to see their brother this way. We were sitting with him at one of the dining tables when he suddenly got up and went back to his room.

John and I went to see Marshall on Christmas morning. We brought goodies and tried to make small talk. I went back alone later that evening. I told Marshall all about Christmas day and told him he had presents waiting for him back home. Then I told Marsh that his uncle Alan was restoring an old pedal car from the 1930s. Marshall suddenly smiled and asked, "How is Uncle Al?" I talked some more, so happy to get a response out of him. He even ate a piece of chocolate that I brought him. It was encouraging.

I visited Marshall the next morning and brought a Medicaid application to have him sign it. I handed him the pen and told him that we needed to get the papers signed so that his hospital stay would be paid for. He held the point against the paper where I placed it, but he could not write. We needed to expedite this, so I placed my hand over his, and guided the pen. He was incapable of checking off the menu selections, but I cheerfully named all of his choices anyway, hoping to spark some interest. He gave no preference, so I marked it for him.

On December 27, when I inquired about Marshall at the nurse's station, Marshall's nurse, Bea, said she had to give Marshall an Ativan for anxiety. This surprised me although I didn't inquire further. I hadn't witnessed any type of anxiety from Marshall since he had been admitted.

On John's and my sixteenth wedding anniversary, December 28, we visited Marshall together. His nurse Mary told us that Marshall answered appropriately for the first time since his admittance. This was great news! And then Marshall unexpectedly asked me if there were any stars in the sky. This was such a sweet and simple question that I blinked back my tears. The things we take for granted!

I visited Marshall at noon and again at five in the afternoon on the twenty-ninth. I was so surprised to see a familiar face from our church. It was Joanne, and she was helping out in behavioral meds for the evening and was his assigned nurse. After Marshall smiled and hugged me good-bye—yes, he actually gave me a hug—Joanne and I sat in the dining area and visited for a long while. I was so grateful to her.

On Wednesday, January 3, a court hearing was held in the hospital. I sat next to Marshall with my hand resting on his arm. There was a large conference table that dominated the room. At the far end of the table sat the judge and court reporter. Next to them was Dr. Mattingly. It was decided that Marshall's stay would be extended an additional twenty-one days so he could become stabilized on the medication and function appropriately before being allowed to leave. I visited Marshall every day, trying not to disrupt our routine at home. Life at home consisted of piano lessons, Tae Kwon Do, pack meetings, car service, a mammogram, my sister Pat's ankle surgery, Pinewood Derby weigh-in, etc.

I had an appointment with Dr. Mattingly on January 9 to discuss Marshall's progress. Marshall was improving and could possibly be released sooner than the twenty-one-day extension period. Marshall had stated to both Dr. Mattingly and me that he wanted to come home.

January 15, 2007 marked a new beginning! Marshall was released from St. Joseph Hospital. I was filled with joy and optimism. I just wanted to hug him and watch him thrive. The nurses were terrific, and I thanked all of them. A social worker told me that it would just be a matter of days and she was certain that Marshall's application for Medicaid would be approved. He was discharged with two prescriptions that needed to be filled on the way home. I drove through Walgreen's and was told that without insurance, his Zyprexa Zydis 20 mg and Lexapro 20 mg would cost $1000 a month. I handed them my credit card and purchased the medication.

When we got home, I faxed all Marshall's hospital records from St. Joseph to the VA for review:

> V.A. Triage 1/17/07
> Enclosed you will find additional medical evidence for my son Marshall Robert Fink.
> While awaiting approval for compensation and disability from the VA, it became necessary to have our son Marshall involuntarily committed to St. Joseph Hospital in St. Charles, Missouri. He had become alarmingly withdrawn and stopped eating entirely. I feared for

his life and obtained a court order to have him taken to the hospital.

He was cared for by Greg Mattingly, MD and was in the hospital from 12/21/06 until his discharge on 01/15/07. He will require medication for the remainder of his life, which is extremely vital for his health and is also exceedingly costly.

Please review the enclosed evidence for compensation and disability.

Marshall served his country and now desperately needs their help. Please give this case immediate consideration.

Sincerely,

Shirlee Gentles

cc Donn Herring (attorney guardianship)

On January 18, 2007, we received the good news that the Missouri Department of Social Services approved benefits, which meant that Marshall's hospital stay would be covered. To say I was relieved was an understatement.

HONORABLE DISCHARGE

Slowly, steadily, and gradually, my son returned. Marshall started popping into his brother's room every day, and they would gently wrestle around. He adored James. In all the photos I have of my two boys, Marshall always has his arm around his little brother's shoulders, as if to protect him.

Marshall started to open up to me. More than anything in the world, Marshall wanted to return to the navy. He'd say to me, "Mom, when they see me, they'll realize their mistake and take me back."

I said, "Marshall, instead of dwelling on that, let's write

down all your qualifications." We wrote: navy engineman EN2. Mercury and Evinrude engine certification. The navy had sent him to training programs in Oakland, California, where he learned all about boat engines. Marshall and his dad restored countless cars and motorcycles over the years, engines included. I said, "Let's make a resume, Marsh. Let's see...you were a distinguished military graduate with a GPA of 94.4 percent in your engineering mechanical course. You were an honor graduate with a GPA of 98.13 percent in your engineering common core course. You've successfully completed your outboard motor overhaul courses. You have a letter of special recognition from a superior officer. Let's type all this up in a resume." This really lifted Marshall's spirits and gave him something positive to work on.

On January 23, I proceeded with the guardianship with the intention now of simply overseeing Marshall's assets to pay his debts if the need ever arose.

On January 31, 2007 Marshall had an appointment with Dr. Mattingly. Marsh told me later that it went very well. It was as if his spirit was restored. I sensed a peacefulness about him and was so glad that he willingly went to the doctor and felt comfortable enough to express his feelings with someone.

Marshall and I were sitting at the kitchen counter on February 7, and he wanted to talk about what he experienced in the naval hospital that still haunted him. I was all ears. Marshall said that he was terrified (his word) in the naval hospital. He said that if he refused or cheeked his meds, they tripled the dosage, and he was zombie-like. He said, "We all walked around like zombies, Mom, terrified of experimentation." He said, "People came through the walls, Mom, and came toward me, showing razor-sharp, pointed teeth!" He said, "The nurses joked about all the patients being so drugged-up." He said, "Remember *One Flew over the Cuckoo's Nest*?" He said, "When we left the hospital, they told me (made me promise) *never* to discuss my naval hospitalization with anyone." Instead of laughing this off though, as if he knew better now, he waited to see how I would react.

I said, "Well, you were most likely sedated and were hallucinating while your meds were being adjusted." He told me that a female patient was escorted into a private room. She emerged much later with an incision and sutures on her skull, the incision running down her forehead. He insisted that this was true and that he knew they had experimented on her. I tried to reassure him that in his condition at the time his perception was distorted. He really was not buying what I was telling him, but he did drop the subject.

He said, "I didn't apply for disability while transitioning out of the military because I didn't want my mental disorder made public." Then he told me it was important to him to get his official discharge DD214 form reissued to read honorable instead of "Other than honorable." He said, "I ran away, Mom. We all wanted to run away."

Marshall did continue to concern me, but for the most part, he was improving. It was just good to hear him talk again. We withdrew our petition for guardianship. The lawyer said we could always start the proceedings later if need be.

On February 17, 2007 Marshall asked me to go with him to see a 1994 Toyota truck that he saw an advertisement for. He liked the truck, and he purchased it. The owner and Marshall talked about his military service, and when Marshall told him about his boat engine certification, the seller said, "You should check with Marine Max. Perhaps they're hiring." It was a great piece of advice because Marshall took his résumé to Marine Max, which was approximately ten miles from our house, and he was hired as a marine mechanic!

They were mostly good days after that, with a few exceptions. Out of the blue, Marshall said, "I mean, what's happening to me? When I was in the ER at St. Joseph Hospital, the nurse was just pumping air into my veins, trying to kill me!" That same day he said, "When I see the movie *We Are Marshall* advertised, I think they're talking about me!"

Marshall's first day at Marine Max/Port Arrowhead was a real milestone. It was March 6, 2007, and I was filled with optimism. I knew this was just what Marshall needed for his self-esteem. Maybe now he'd give up the notion, or hope, that the navy would want him back!

By March 8, we still had not heard from the VA. Marshall received a letter from Social Security in regard to the disability claim. The letter stated that they were writing because they had not received records from Balboa Hospital, Naval Medical Center.

I called the Naval Medical Center. They never received that request due to "Wrong Zip code." I called the Social Security administration back to have the State of Missouri request a records transfer. Marshall had become my full-time job.

We received three to four correspondences from the Social Security administration. One letter stated:

> We need more information to decide if we can pay you SSI. Therefore, it is important that you do the following:

-Sign and date the enclosed form(s). Return the form(s), and this letter in enclosed envelope.

Now that Marshall was working, he contacted a hearing officer for a disability determination at the Social Security office to inform them that he wanted to withdraw his application for benefits because he now had a job and was doing fine on his medication.

On March 10, Marshall told me that he had a bad day, and my heart sank. He said, "I forgot to reinforce a boat on the trailer while towing it, and although nothing bad happened, it could have!" He said, "I'm just tired, not used to working. That's all." But I could tell he was worried. He said that his boss did notice that it wasn't properly secured.

Later that same night, I questioned Marshall about the empty J&B Scotch bottle I found in his room. He's not supposed to drink while on psych meds. He told me that he has one small glass every evening plus two to three beers. I also found two boxes (twenty-one capsules each) of Diurex, a caffeine/water capsule/weight loss drug, in his drawer. Six were missing.

A couple days later, I gave back Marshall's knives when he asked for them. We had removed everything that was potentially dangerous from his room when he was hospitalized (we never did find the gun). He had a small knife collection, mostly from Boy Scouts. I told Marshall that we thought it was necessary to remove them because we worried about his safety. Marshall said, "Yea, yea, yea," impatiently. In other words, he didn't want us to bring up his disorder. That was very clear.

On March 19, I could hear Marshall moving about in his bedroom, which was right below our room. It was one thirty in the morning, and I knew he had to get up for work the next day. I went downstairs to ask him if he took his Zyprexa. He said, "Not yet, but don't worry. I've been taking my snake oil. Just don't check up on me, okay?" It was clear he didn't want his mother looking over his shoulder. I was reminded that a facet of bipolar disorder is the belief that you no longer need your meds.

I wrote all of my concerns down on paper to share with Dr. Mattingly before Marshall's next appointment on April 30. I wanted to be prepared. I also made a copy of a newspaper article for Dr. Mattingly titled "Many Returning from Wars Face New Foe: Homelessness" (Addiction and mental health issues get much of the blame for the growing problem. And mental illness and addiction are major reasons they have no jobs and no place to live). Also cited were relationships broken by long and repeated tours of duty.

I called the VA on April 9, 2007 and spoke to the patient advocate, Cynthia Corkery. She advised me to write a letter to Senator Kit Bond because his office handled VA issues. She told me to write a letter of explanation and attach a copy of Marshall's military files, his DD214 (discharge paper), and the most recent progress report from Dr. Mattingly. We only had three weeks to try to get something resolved because Marshall's state aid would end at that time. I didn't want there to be any break in his medication regimen, so I composed a letter and copied all his military files.

Dr. Mattingly provided the accompanying progress report:

> April 10, 2007
> To Whom It May Concern:
> Marshall Fink is a patient under my medical supervision for his ongoing treatment of bipolar disorder. Marshall is responding well to his cur-

> rent medications which consist of ongoing medical treatment. He would become very ill without these medications and needs.
> Sincerely,
> Greg Mattingly, MD

I faxed all the forms to the patient advocate, thanking her for her kindness. I told her that prior to her assistance, I was unsure of which avenue to pursue and was running out of time.

On April 11, 2007 I was contacted by Janna Worsham from Kit Bond's office. She faxed me a privacy authorization form, asking Marshall to fill it out for the VA inquiry. Under "Problem" Marshall wrote:

> Please determine disability compensation. I applied in September 06. Please expedite due to disability received while in active military service as I cannot afford paying $1000 a month for medication. I also wish to change my DD214 status to honorable due to my exemplary performance.

I faxed the completed inquiry that included Marshall's statement to Ms. Worsham. She sent the inquiry to the VA through the senator's office. She told me that even though Marshall's DD214 read other than honorable, the VA could still provide services. She told me to allow them to determine benefits for Marsh first, before pursuing a status change through the board for correction of naval records.

On April 13, 2007 I talked to Richard Ivy from the regional VA office. He said that his regional office *does* have the authority to overturn Marshall's other than honorable status. He told me that what he needed from me and what would "carry the most weight" is a letter from Dr. Mattingly outlining:

- Behavioral traits of bipolar disorder that could lead someone to go AWOL.
- Is it the doctor's opinion that if Marshall was treated in the military for this disorder, could he have been helped or "fixed" (his words).

Mr. Ivy asked if Dr. Mattingly could review Marshall's service record. Once he received that letter from the doctor, he would review the discharge status, and we could then apply for a discharge upgrade.

Dr. Mattingly graciously complied and wrote:

To Whom It May Concern,

Marshall Fink is a patient under my medical supervision for the treatment of bipolar disorder. He is responding well to his current medication. Marshall would become very ill without these medications and ongoing medical treatment.

Listed below are some of the behaviors individuals may display if diagnosed with bipolar disorder.

1. *Inflated self-esteem or grandiosity*
2. *Decrease need for sleep*
3. *More talkative than usual or pressure to keep talking*
4. *Flight of ideas or subjective experience that thoughts are racing*
5. *Distractibility*
6. *Increase in goal-directed activity or psychomotor agitation*
7. *Excessive involvement in pleasurable activities that have a high potential for painful consequences*

Sincerely,
Greg Mattingly, MD

While this letter did not answer the two questions posed, it would prove to be critical in the decision.

I drove Marshall to downtown St. Louis on April 16 for his appointment with Richard Ivy at the VA. Mr. Ivy wanted to meet with Marshall personally before making any decisions about changing his discharge status. I thought the meeting went well, but Mr. Ivy gave no indication at that time of what the outcome would be.

On the same day that Marshall met with Richard Ivy at the VA regional office downtown, I received a letter from the VA Medical Center at Jefferson Barracks:

> *Dear Ms. Gentles,*
>
> *We received information from the VA Regional Office, St. Louis, Missouri, informing us that your son does not meet the required eligibility to receive medical care at the VA Medical Center. Their records show the discharge you received from active duty military service from January 17, 2002, to April 11, 2006, was other than honorable and a bar to VA benefits.*
>
> *If you have any questions or concerns regarding this decision, please contact the eligibility office, Tuesday through Friday, from 8:00 a.m. to 3:00 p.m.*
>
> *Sincerely,*
> *Renee Collins*
> *Health Administration Officer*

One hand did not know what the other is doing! Marshall received the following a letter from the senator's office on the seventeenth of April:

> *Dear Mr. Fink,*
>
> *Thank you for your recent letter expressing concern about the difficulties you have experienced in obtaining disability compensation for your*

> bipolar condition. I understand your concern about this matter.
>
> In response to your request, I have asked the department of veteran's affairs to initiate a congressional inquiry into this matter. I look forward to notifying you of the outcome of their inquiry.
>
> My office and I appreciate the opportunity to be of assistance to you.
>
> Sincerely,
> Kit Bond
> United States Senator

On April 24, my new primary doctor recommended a sleep study, and so I spent the night at the hospital.

> Mrs. Shirlee Gentles is a fifty-one-year-old female seen on April 24, 2007, on referral by Dr. Kim for further evaluation of these abnormal nocturnal behaviors. Mrs. Gentles recalled a relatively benign pattern of sleep until approximately twelve months ago when there was a dramatic increase in stress. Her older son, a soldier serving in the armed forces, went missing. He apparently developed bipolar disorder and was eventually returned to the states for medical care, including hospitalization. His course over the last twelve months has been quite complex, with many seemingly abrupt and unpredictable course changes and events. Some aspects of his recent life seem unknown or confusing to Mrs. Gentles. This stress was aggravated by his dishonorable discharge, against which his mother has been fighting in an effort to get him reclassified as an honorable discharge. Over this time, she

has been his primary caregiver and seemingly sole proponent. She also suspects a biological change. Beginning in the fall of 2006, she entered her peri-menopausal period and went on hormone replacement in October.

Despite all of these events, she feels she has maintained a relatively good mood. She does not feel depressed or anxious, despite the suspicions of many previous physicians with whom she has consulted. At night, however, a dramatic change occurs. She develops a shaky, head quivering, vibration-like tremor that is both an internal sensation and visible. She describes teeth chattering, head movement, and muscle twitching. She becomes dyspneic. She can hear this vibration. She likens it to "my nerve endings are all vibrating." She was initially scared that all of these symptoms indicated a process that was "going to kill me." She now resigns herself to it, is less fearful, and eventually falls asleep despite the symptoms. She will then wake up intermittently through the night with the same sensations. Hormone replacement has not resulted in a significant improvement. She has met with an ENT who carried out an evaluation for vertigo. She would wake up with vertigo, nausea, and muscle twitching. She met with two neurologists. Their impression was that she was suffering from anxiety of depression and recommended antidepressants that either resulted in side effects or aggravated what she describes as night time anxiety and panic. She has recently moved from her previous primary care doctor to Dr. Kim for reevaluation. An endocrinologist consultation is scheduled.

Impressions:

I strongly suspect Mrs. Gentles has a nocturnal panic disorder. I have a low suspicion that this represents a seizure disorder. A sleep related anxiety disorder/panic attacks is uncommon, but is not rare. She is interested in obtaining objective validation that she is having these nocturnal spells. I think a polysomnography is reasonable to collect evidence. I have discussed a trial of clonazepam with her briefly under the hypothesis that this medication will be helpful and tolerable regardless of whether she is suffering from anxiety or a sleep related movement disorder.

Off the record, he mentioned something about post-traumatic stress disorder.

I returned later on the twenty-fourth for a polysomnogram to complete the evaluation for atypical nocturnal events associated with palpitations, shortness of breath, anxiety, and tremor.

Findings:

"No sleep apnea. Mild to moderate increase in number of limb movements, nine arousals per hour."

I relayed my concerns about Marshall.

On the thirtieth Marshall had an appointment with Dr. Mattingly and returned home in very good spirits.

Then, on May 1, 2007 I met with Richard Ivy at the VA and received the most glorious news I'd ever heard in my life. Marshall's discharge status was changed to read 'Honorable.'

The overview read:

> *The veteran was admitted to the Naval Medical Center on September 22, 2005, based on odd behavior patterns. On November 8, 2005, he was diagnosed with bipolar disorder, single manic episode, moderate with mood congruent psychotic features, schizotypal traits, and occupational and social problems. Based on this evidence, the medical board was of the opinion that the service member was unable to perform further military service as a result of a disability and that disability did not exist prior to entry in the service and, therefore, is considered to have incurred in or have been aggravated by a period of military service. Based on the evidence of record, his military service is considered to be acceptable and honest, faithful and meritorious. Therefore, his military service from January 17, 2002, to April 11, 2006, is considered to be honorable and, therefore, is entitled to full right and privileges of VA benefits."*

These were the sweetest words Marshall and I had ever heard!

LAST PHOTO

On May 7, it was still crucial to Marshall to appeal to the naval council. He so wanted national approval for status change, in addition to the locally-approved status change. In his mind, it was the last hurdle, and it meant everything to him. Marshall applied for "Correction of Military Record." He wrote:

> Naval Council of Personnel Boards 5/7/07
> 720 Kennon Street, S.E.
> Room 309 (NDRB)
> Washington Navy Yard, DC
> 20374-5023
> I, Marshall Robert Fink, do hereby request a status upgrade on my DD214 to read honorable.
> Due to the mental illness, bipolar disorder, which was out of my control, I went AWOL as I was being processed out of the navy. After a lengthy and thorough process, a review panel here at the St. Louis VA Regional Office overturned my "other than honorable" status to "honorable."
> I am asking the board to please review these findings, and if you agree with them, send me a new DD214 that states my discharge as honorable.
> Thank you for your consideration.
> Sincerely,
> Marshall Robert Fink

This letter was mailed with attached medical records from both the Naval Medical Center and St. Joseph's Hospital. He also included my impassioned letter to Senator Kit Bond, Dr. Mattingly's letter outlining the manifestations of bipolar illness, his letters of recognition, and his Good Conduct Award.

May 14, Marshall had an appointment with Ms. Henderson with the VA to enroll for healthcare. The worksheet indicated a request for meds and a request for a new patient psych consult. A Dr. R prescribed Citalopram Hydrobromide 40 mg (take one every AM) which replaced the Lexapro. Olanzapine 20mg was also prescribed (take a half tab once daily). Ms. Henderson scheduled Marshall's appointment with Dr. J, a psychiatrist at Jefferson Barracks Hospital for June 18, 2007.

Marshall had three appointments on Wednesday, May 23 for compensation and pension at John Cochran VA Hospital downtown, scheduled an hour apart. Mr. Ivy told us that after these appointments, a review by rating specialists would be done at the regional office.

The Department of Veteran's Affairs sent a letter to Senator Bond, which was then forwarded to us from the Senator's office:

> *Dear Senator Bond: May 31, 2007*
> *Thank you for your inquiry dated April 16, 2007, on behalf of Mr. Marshall R. Fink.*
> *Mr. Fink has a claim pending for service-connected compensation for bipolar disorder and a claim for non-service-connected pension to include special monthly pension benefits. On May 2, 2007, we transferred Mr. Fink's file to the Department of Veteran's Affairs Medical Center in St. Louis to schedule him for an examination. They will notify Mr. Fink of the date and time to report. Once Mr. Fink's file is returned to our office, a rating specialist will review the entire file, including any new evidence submitted, and*

render a decision. We will notify both you and Mr. Fink of the final decision.

If Mr. Fink wishes to have his DD form 214, certificate of release of discharge from active duty, changed, he may complete the enclosed DD form 149, application for correction of military record under the provisions of title 10, US code, section 1552, and return it to the appropriate address on the back of the form.

If Mr. Fink has additional questions, he may call our toll free number. A veteran's service representative will be happy to assist him.

I appreciate your continued interest on behalf of Missouri veterans and their dependents.

Sincerely yours,

J. David Unterwagner

Acting Director

On June 11, 2007 Marshall had first appointment at the VA St. Charles Clinic for lab work.

Marshall received a letter from Senator Bond:

Dear Mr. Fink: June 13, 2007

Thank you for contacting my office. I am pleased to report to you with good news.

Enclosed you will find reply to my office from the department of veteran's affairs regional office. This agency reports that the problem has been resolved in obtaining your entitlement to service-connected benefits for your bipolar condition.

I am pleased to have the opportunity to help and hope that you will contact my office in the future if I may be of further assistance.

Sincerely,

Christopher (Kit)
S. Bond

On June 18, 2007 Marshall had an appointment with psychiatrist Dr. J at Jefferson Barracks Medical Center. Dr. J recommended cutting the Zyprexa to half the doseage with the possibility of eliminating it altogether. Even though Marshall's status allowed him to be seen by a VA doctor, I still wanted him to see Dr. Mattingly.

I talked to Sylvia Ivy (Richard's wife) who works at the VA hospital in the release of information department. She requested (and received) records from Dr. Mattingly to scan into their system, so that Dr. C. J. could review them.

In addition, I made copies of records from both hospitalizations for Dr. J and, I wrote the following memo:

> Dr. C. J., 6/20/07
>
> *I am writing on behalf of my son, Marshall R. Fink who you saw in your office on 6/18/07.*
>
> *Enclosed are Marshall's medical records from his hospitalization at the Naval Medical Center in San Diego, dated 09/05.*
>
> *Also enclosed are records from his most recent hospitalization at St. Joseph Health Center here in St. Charles, Missouri, dated 12/06.*
>
> *Marshall has been under the care of Dr. Greg Mattingly. Please call Dr. Mattingly at your earliest convenience to discuss Marshall's care and prescription regimen.*
>
> *Sincerely,*
>
> *Shirlee Gentles*

I drove to Jefferson Barrack's Medical Center and dropped off the records for Dr. J.

On July 23, 2007 Marshall had an appointment with Dr. Mattingly. Marshall told Dr. Mattingly about his recent visit with his new VA doctor. Marshall smiled when he told me about this meeting with Mattingly. I loved listening to him, and it was gratifying to see him acting so happy and contented. He told me that Dr. Mattingly had not heard from Dr. J yet.

Marshall received a letter from social services on July 27 stating, "This is your last day of coverage. This action was taken because you voluntarily requested that your case can be closed."

On July 28, My bedside notes read: "Tachycardia, irregular heartbeat, heart pain, vibrate, tremors, chills, flared nostrils, back pain between the shoulder blades, left arm weakness, labored breathing, *worn out* in a.m. Completely, utterly exhausted!"

On August 4, 2007 Marshall was doing very well on a daily basis and we met his dad, Dick, in Bloomington, IL. Marshall was going to stay with his dad for a few days!

On August 7, I interviewed with Dr. Simo, a plastic surgeon and owner of Spaderma. I was hired as an R.N. (medical esthetician). I was so excited to start my new job in my chosen field!

On August 8, Marshall was in the garage moving a Harley Davidson engine toward the corner, and that reminded me about the 1960 Triumph motorcycle he was going to sell back in 2005. He told me that while he was hiding out in Yuma, Arizona, his storage unit was broken into, and someone stole the motorcycle. He said, "The owner of the storage facility told me that he was not liable for my loss." Someone most certainly profited from that misfortune. I meant to, but never followed up on this. After all, I was the one who called to have his storage units opened up when I feared he was hurt and locked inside one of them.

It was Marshall's twenty-sixth birthday on August 11, 2007, and I called Marine Max to ask if it would be okay to take a birthday cake to the business, and they said yes. I had a cake decorated with a Sea Ray boat on it, and it was a big hit with Marshall's coworkers. It was good to see him interact.

My brother Mike and his family were visiting us on Marshall's birthday. Marsh was so happy to hang out with his uncle. Since returning home from the navy, he hadn't contacted his old friends. Perhaps it was out of embarrassment or low self-esteem, but his only friends now were the guys from work. He was tuning up the engine on the used dirt bike he bought recently, because it didn't run when he got it. He was showing it to his uncle Mike and asked him if he'd like to ride it, which Mike did. Marshall was getting ready to go dirt biking for the day with the guys at work. Six months later, Mike would write about that last encounter he had with his nephew in a poignant and insightful letter.

Marshall had been actively looking at houses with the intention of buying his first house.

He was interested in the St. Louis Hills neighborhood downtown, off of Hampton. He was particularly fond of Pernod St. He had been doing a lot of searching online and was in contact with a real estate agent. One day he took my mom and me to see a few houses he really liked to get our opinion. He was considering making an offer on one.

On October 22, 2007, Marshall had another appointment with Dr. Mattingly. As far as I was concerned, these appointments were now just for maintenance purposes. Marshall was acting like his old self and I was counting my blessings.

For James's twelfth birthday on November 21, 2007,

John, Marshall, James, and I went to Kobe Japanese Steakhouse (James's favorite). This is the last picture I have of Marshall. He looks calm, content, even reserved, but older than his years. It's as if he's experienced much in his young life. There is no hint yet of what is to come.

On November 30, John and I were going out for dinner, and I asked Marshall if he would take James to McDonald's. Marshall said sure. I thanked him, and he looked at me as if to say, "No big deal." Two brothers going out for fast food. So normal, I had to pinch myself. I could not wipe the smile off my face all evening!

SLIPPING AWAY

It had been a year since Marshall was taken to the hospital for treatment, and on December 21, 2007 I was starting to get concerned about him. He told me, "Mom, I'm thinking about giving all my money away to charity."

I said, "Son, that is noble of you, but you've been house hunting, and you'll need money to buy a house, won't you?" I said, "How about calling some friends, Marsh. Do you want to have some of your old friends over to the house?"

He answered, "Too many friends are dangerous." How that statement saddened me. I immediately flashed back to all the times his friends filled this house. I thought of his core group of male friends; JC, Scott, Dustin, Matt, Ben, and Chris. They would oftentimes all cram into his bedroom to play Nintendo while tossing a basketball back and forth. Once, when a couple of the boys dove onto Marshall's futon to wrestle, it cracked from the weight. Long since repaired, that futon now sits as a reminder of the friendships and comraderie my son had during his high school years.

I also observed that there had been uneaten food in the lunches I packed for him, and he was getting thinner.

I wrapped Christmas presents for Marshall to take up to his dad's on the twenty-second. He was getting ready to drive up there for the holiday. Lately, I had been finding empty beer bottles lined up next to his bed after he left for work in the morning. I'd also seen an empty glass that smelled of hard liquor. He must have been stopping on his way home from work to buy this because we didn't keep beer in the house. I called Dick to state my concerns and asked him to give me his opinion when he saw Marshall.

On December 27, Marshall returned from his dad's house. He had an appointment with Dr. J at Jefferson Barracks VA Hospital. Marshall told Dr. J that he was having headaches recently and was often tired. Dr. J told Marshall that the Zyprexa was not the right prescription for him due to his lab results. He also told Marshall that he would gradually take him off of his meds, stating, "Maybe you don't need meds anymore." I was certain that Marshall misunderstood what the doctor said. I was sure that Dr. J was merely adjusting Marshall's medication and would coordinate his care with Dr. Mattingly, so I dismissed it at the time. Later that evening, Marshall was acting odd. He told me that when he was driving up to his dad's, "I could really focus. My senses were so sharp, and it was surreal when I was driving. It was like…*wow*." That statement and the euphoria in his voice caused more than a little alarm. Then I noticed in Marshall's car that he brought back my containers of cookies, which were intended for his dad and Aunt Kathy. I questioned him about it, and he said, "They didn't need it. They had enough food."

I asked, "How did Blake and Brynn like their gifts?"

He said, "I wasn't going to give them their gifts cause they had a enough presents. But then Blake found the packages and said, 'What are these?'" It was a disturbing conversation. Then, Marshall imitated Blake's young voice. He said, "Thank you, Marshall, for the presents." Then he repeated this statement in a childlike voice, which sounded very creepy.

And I thought, *Please, God, not again.*

That night I lay awake, listening for Marshall to come

upstairs. I could hear that he was awake. He kept opening the patio door to go outside and smoke a cigarette. Around 2:00 a.m., I went downstairs and asked him if he took his meds. He told me he'd take them later. I told him that I saw a new billboard on Highway 270 earlier in the day, and it was an advertisement for a Marine Max boat show that was coming up. He asked for the location of the billboard, and I told him. When I went back upstairs, I heard Marshall leave the house and drive off.

He returned almost an hour later, and I met him in the kitchen. I said, "Son, it's so late. Where did you go?"

He said, "I drove all over, and I never saw that billboard you were talking about." I was astounded that he felt the need to go check this out! I asked if he would be helping out at the boat show. He answered, "Living the boating dream," which happens to be Marine Max's motto.

On December 29, I called both Dick and then Kathy to ask how Marshall was acting when he was up there for Christmas. Dick told me that Marshall was acting strangely. Kathy said he was very quiet. I thought, *Oh no! Please God…I'm begging you…don't let this happen to Marsh again!*

The next evening, I went down to Marshall's room and asked him not to drink so much. There were twelve empty bottles lined up next to his bed. I told him that he shouldn't be mixing alcohol with his meds. His response shocked me, "Get [expletive] and die!" Observing my shocked expression, he repeated, "And DIE" with more emphasis.

I said, "Marshall, you cannot talk to me like that! Now come on, I'm getting concerned about you, that's all."

He said, "I'll just shoot myself. Alcohol is good for you. It's water that's bad."

I said, "Marsh, that's not right. You're not making sense."

He said, "Are you going to make me get a lobotomy?"

By now, I was starting to panic. But I tried hard not to show it. I was wondering if he sounded this bizarre at work. He had been getting up for work every day. Surely someone would have called me if Marshall made comments like that at work. I decided that I had to talk to Dr. Mattingly before Marshall's next appointment on January 8.

By January 1, 2008, Marshall was not sleeping at all from what I could hear by his rummaging around. I would lay in bed with one eye trained on my open doorway. I was on high alert, listening for the soft *click* that warned me when Marshall was coming upstairs. We had a dinner party scheduled here at the house on the fourth. I prayed that Marshall improved by then. But he was incommunicative and getting thinner. He still stopped in James's room after work, briefly, to wrestle with him, but had ceased doing anything else with his brother since before Christmas. I was getting more worried each day.

On the third I opened up our liquor cabinet to get an assortment out for the party the next day and each and every bottle was empty! There were twelve empty bottles in all! I lined up all the empties on the kitchen counter and took a photo. I called Marshall upstairs to explain. He just stared at the bottles and said nothing. I asked, "Marshall, when did you do this? How long has this been going on? This is a lot of alcohol, Marshall, and you've been sneaking this from under our noses!" He went back downstairs without answering me.

I called Dr. Mattingly's office to voice my concerns and give him a heads-up before Marshall's scheduled appointment on Monday.

On the fourth of January, we were having our dinner party and Marshall came home from work just as we finished eating. He walked past a couple of our guests toward James's room. I saw a surprised look on Beth's face when she saw him. She glanced my way thinking, perhaps, I would introduce the two of them. But, he breezed by her, and I didn't want to stop him. I didn't trust what would come out of his mouth, and I was certain that whatever he said would undoubtedly prove to be inappropriate. He had been unpredictable and got easily agitated.

He was out of James's room in a matter of minutes then retreated to his bedroom for the remainder of the night. Once again, after the guests left, I heard Marshall's television on all night and the patio door slamming closed every twenty minutes when he went outside to smoke.

Marshall had his appointment with Dr. Mattingly on the seventh. I was so relieved thinking, *Okay, now he's going to start improving. We'll get him back on track soon.* Dr. Mattingly stated to me the previous week that he was going to address Marshall's drinking.

But by January 8, Marshall wasn't getting any better. He was still retreating to his room after work. He would not talk to us. His belt was on the tightest notch to hold his pants on. He did not eat any of the lunch I packed for him. I hoped that he had listened to Dr. Mattingly's advice, but I was a little doubtful. I was hoping to see steady improvement. When I went downstairs to check on him, Marshall pointed to the door and said, "Get the hell out of my room!" Then he pointed a finger at his head and made a gunshot sound. I prayed with renewed vigor and intent. I prayed for peace for Marshall.

TRAGEDY

On that last week of Marshall's life, I immersed myself in prayer every night. I knelt by the bathroom counter praying and then continued praying when I got into bed. Up until this week, I often prayed, asking God to heal Marshall. But as I watched Marshall going downhill as the week progressed, I could feel the situation becoming desperate. My prayers now became a plea for peace. I prayed for an end to his turmoil, his torment. I wanted to see that tortured expression of his change to one of complete serenity. I wanted nothing more than for Marshall's demeanor to be replaced by a calm contentment. Blissful peace—I could feel it. My breathing slowed. There was nothing between God and me, and I knew with my life that He was listening.

    I fell asleep reciting the names of all those I was grateful for. I went through a mental list—my sister Pat, my brothers, my mom, James, John, Terri, my girlfriends—naming everyone that I could think of until sleep overtook me, my hands still clasped in prayer. That is, until I'd wake with a sudden jolt and stare at the doorway, cocking my head to listen closely for footsteps, hoping Marshall wasn't coming to harm us.

    On January 9, Marshall left for work. I took James to school, and I went to John's office to help out. That evening I walked into Marshall's room with a cheery hello. I asked how his day went, and he said that he wasn't able to finish working on a boat repair. He stated that his boss told him the job should take a few hours, but Marsh worked on it for days. He looked confused. Then he said, "I can't talk about work—confidentiality." He became giddy.

I said, "Marsh, what do you mean, you can't talk about work?" He pointed toward the door and told me to get out. I said, "Come on, Marsh. It's okay to talk to me. I'm interested in what you do."

He said, "I'm quitting my job. I can't work for a place called Marine Max. It sounds like Mad Max. I'm planning my strategy." I was getting nauseous. I was thinking that no one should have to witness the rantings of a beloved son, a son who was losing his mind. At 12:30 a.m., I asked him to please take his meds so he could get some sleep. He pointed his finger at his head and kept "shooting" himself every time I said anything. He said, "You take the [expletive] pills. Leave or I'll shoot you!"

I went up to bed and laid there shaking, writing, and not sleeping for one blessed minute.

Marshall got up and left for work the next morning, which was unbelievable to me. *How is he acting at work?* I wondered. *Why hasn't anyone called me from his job? Is he functioning okay there?* I knew that couldn't be possible. He was just at the doctor's on Monday, three days ago. *When will I start to see an improvement? Is it possible that he will improve?*

I met my friend Terri at the bread company. I needed to talk. I told Terri that if Marshall wasn't better by Monday I would be forced to start proceedings for another involuntary confinement, a process that made me physically ill to think about. I knew I had no choice and was giving him until Monday.

On January 11, 2008, John left for work. I tried to wake Marshall. He had fourteen empty bottles of beer next to the bed. *Dear God, help me. Help Marshall, please.* He said, "I'm not going to work today." I quickly took James to school and returned to Marshall's room.

I said, "Marsh, get up. You have to go to work."

He said, "No, I'm not." Now I was fearful that he'd lose the one thing that made him happy. He was thrilled when he got that job! Surely his bizarre behavior and now missing work would result in his dismissal. I called Marine Max. In a desperate effort to buy him some more time, I told them that Marshall was sick and wouldn't be in today. I called Dr. Mattingly's office and told them Marshall was getting worse. Crystal said Dr. Mattingly would be out of the office until Monday. Now, I knew I'd have to have him hospitalized if he couldn't get this under control.

Marshall was still in his room when John, James, and I went to a trivia night at our church. When we returned home, I went directly to Marshall's room to see how he was doing. When I knocked and opened the door, I was met with what can only be described as a caged animal. Marshall, who had been standing by his dresser, came toward me with fury. I could see his neck veins bulging.

I said, "Son, are you all right?" What came out of his mouth was more like a grunt as he chest-butted me out of his doorway. I blurted out, "Oh my God, Marshall! You're scaring me. Please, honey, stop it!" His face was contorted in rage. He was in a full-blown psychotic rage.

He said, "I'll kill you!" Then pushed past me and walked out of the patio door.

I ran to John's office and blurted to John that Marshall was psychotic and was threatening to kill me. I said, "I'm terrified of him!"

John yelled, "Go upstairs, and call 911."

As he said this, we both looked outside his open window and saw Marshall pacing and looking in at us. I knew he heard John's command. John and I both exited his office at the same time and were going to head upstairs when Marshall came walking back inside at a fast pace right toward us. He held up both arms as if holding a shotgun, made a cocking gun sound, and aimed his imaginary gun at my forehead then said, "I could blow both of you away with one shot!"

John said, "Marshall, Marshall, Marshall!" with urgency and fear in his voice, all of us now on hyper adrenaline. "Don't talk like that. Shirlee, go!"

I ran upstairs and grabbed the kitchen phone and slipped into the laundry room to hide while, at the same time, dialing 911. I said, "My son is threatening to kill us. He's off of his medication and needs to go to the hospital. Come quick!" But Marshall was right there, grabbing the phone out of my hand. He started to slam it on the counter. I ran into the kitchen, and he came after me. I faced him and pleaded with him to "Stop! Please stop, Marsh! You're scaring me!" He began chest-butting me, pushing me backward. I tried to stay on my feet, walking backward around the kitchen island, while he kept on chest-butting me and grunting. I ran for the kitchen door and opened it.

He said, "You're not going anywhere," and closed it. I opened it again and ran out through the garage as fast as I could run. He came out after me and grabbed me in the driveway and said, "You're not going anywhere." Then he pushed me back into the garage. He kept pushing me toward the kitchen, and I leaned up against a car to face him.

I begged him, "Please, Marshall, stop it. You're hurting me, and I love you. You're scaring me, and I just want to get you some help."

He grabbed me again, and I heard John groan from

the doorway. John pleaded, "Marshall, don't hurt your mother." This distracted Marshall momentarily, and I made a run for John. John and I watched in horror as Marshall began slamming his fists through the garage wall. Over and over he punched with all of his strength as plasterboard flew around us in chunks.

I screamed, "Marshall, *please* stop. You're hurting yourself!" We were so shocked as we witnessed this that we stood frozen in fear. In an instant, we both saw him turn to look at us. John and I instinctively tried to close the door to keep Marshall out, but Marshall quickly sensed this and pushed his way in before we could get the door locked. John started to walk toward the steps leading downstairs as I walked backward, Marshall chest-butting me again. I kept pleading with him to stop. He did stop, turned on the sink faucet, and began running his bloody hands under the water. I ran from the kitchen past the stairway, shouting "James, come now!" At that moment, John was just walking up the stairs. I saw that he had a pistol in his right hand, down at his side. James came running out of his room and stood frozen in the hallway, wearing only a shirt and his underwear. I said, "Hurry, come outside now!"

He ran to me, I grabbed his hand, and we fled out the front door after hearing John say, "Marshall, this is loaded, and you're going to listen to us now."

I said, "Let's run as fast as we can." I said, "I'm sorry, James, but your brother is very sick. He's not well, and we have to go to the neighbors!"

We were just past our property when we heard a single gunshot. I knew my neighbors were out of town. We ran down to my friends' house at the end of the block and pounded on the door. No one answered. We went around the back and pounded some more. Still no answer. I kept looking toward our house to see if Marshall was coming to get us. I assumed he had wrestled the gun away from John and it went off, or, God forbid, one of them was hurt! We tried the next door neighbor, and again, no answer. We ran back across the street to Thompsons's house. We pounded, and the door flew open. We leapt inside, and I told Dawn to lock her doors and turn off the lights. I said, "My son is after us."

She said, "Does he know you're here?"

I said I didn't know if he followed us or not. I said, "We heard a gunshot, and I don't know who was hurt." She instructed her son to take James upstairs and get him some pants and socks and play some video games. I said, "Call 911." I then called my friend Terri so she could alert Dr. Mattingly that Marshall needed help. We heard a knock on her back patio door, and we froze.

I said, "Don't answer that. He's here to get us!" We stood against her wall in the hallway, not moving. The knock came again, and Dawn heard her son call out. It wasn't Marshall after all!

I was on the phone now, talking to the 911 operator. I told her that my young son and I fled our house to get away from my older son who was aggressive and psychotic. She told me that a deputy would be there very soon and to stay where I was. Minutes later, Deputy Howze introduced himself. I frantically asked him if my husband was okay. He said that yes, he was not hurt. I was relieved and asked about Marshall. He told me that Marshall had been hurt. I said, "Oh no, will he be okay?"

The deputy said, "I don't know ma'am, but they're working on him now."

I said, "You *must* ask them to take him to St. Joseph Hospital. He's been there before, and his doctor is there."

He said okay. I repeated that I didn't want a mix-up and have him accidently taken to Barnes St. Peters. "It has to be St. Joseph," I told him. "His doctor is there and knows Marshall's history." I was actually relieved that he would now be hospitalized. This meant I didn't even have to start the process of doing another involuntary confinement.

And then there were several police in the room all of a sudden. Detective Tim MacMann introduced himself and asked me if I could tell him what happened this evening. I started to tell them about Marshall, when his mental illness was first diagnosed in 2005, and what we've been doing to get him help. He then introduced me to another detective, and I proceeded to tell them what happened that night. I told them that when we got home and I asked Marshall how he was, he told me to "Get screwed and die." Alarmed and feeling a rising panic, I alerted my husband. I then proceeded to give both detectives a detailed account of all that transpired from the time we arrived home. MacMann asked me if I was afraid for my safety. I told him I was very much afraid for my safety as well as that of my husband and younger son. I said I was certain that Marshall had stopped taking his medication and that he'd been drinking heavily. I told them I discovered a lot of empty liquor bottles. MacMann handed me some paper and asked me to write it all down. I welcomed the opportunity to give them the facts, and I had so much to say. I started to write at a frenzied pace. Page after page I wrote, only pausing to ask how Marshall was and if they'd taken him to the hospital yet. When I finished a page, it was distributed, making the rounds to each and every one of them. They all were very interested in what I had written.

While I wrote, McMann asked if he could talk to James. I gave permission, and he summoned James downstairs. He asked James how he was doing, and James said he was okay. He then asked him if he heard his brother and parent's talking that evening. James said yes. The detective asked if he heard yelling, and again, James answered yes, stating that he heard his brother arguing with his parents. He told the detective that he didn't know what we were arguing about. James stated that I came and got him and told him that his brother was sick. He told MacMann that while we were leaving the house, he heard his brother yelling at his dad. He also told the detective that when we were outside, he heard something that sounded like a shot come from inside the house. When asked, James told him that his brother had been spending most of his time down in his room.

Finally, after almost six pages, I stopped writing. I said, "That's all I have in me and can't write anymore." I asked if my girlfriend Terri arrived, and they said she had and was also providing a written statement. I said, "Can someone please tell me how Marshall is doing and if he is being treated at the hospital yet?"

I was sitting at Dawn's kitchen table, and at that moment, Detective MacMann reached over and placed his hand over mine. We locked eyes, and he said, "I'm so sorry, but your son is dead."

I couldn't believe what I'd just heard, and blurted, "No!" He asked me if it was all right to tell James, and I shook my head, yes. I heard him tell James that his brother was dead and watched as my son wiped his tears. I hugged him from behind and said, "It'll be okay, James. I love you." But I knew it wasn't going to be okay, not for a long time, and I was in a state of shock.

Dawn offered to keep James for the night, and I kissed him good-bye.

Terri had been sitting in her car this whole time, writing down her statement. I was escorted out to her, and we both hugged and cried. Then the two detectives walked us back to my house, which was surrounded by yellow crime scene tape. A few squad cars sat out front. I asked about John, and one of them said, "Your husband was taken in for questioning."

Terri and I entered my house and walked toward the kitchen where a few remaining detectives stood. We were met by our two dogs, and I wondered how they fared during this entire, long evening. Detective Joseph Henke introduced himself, stating he was sorry for my loss. He told me they were keeping John at the jail overnight, and I could call the next day. Detective Henke said, "So you were at Messiah Lutheran tonight? Is Pastor Schult still there?" I told him yes, he was, and he said, "Oh, he's a great guy. He confirmed my kids." Detective Henke was so kind and tried to put me at ease, knowing this must have been a hellish night for all of us. He told me they'd finished processing the house and were done for the night.

I heard a female cop say, "Oh, there's some blood over there by the cabinet." As Terri made her way over to the sink to get some paper towels, Detective Henke asked if there was anything I needed or if I had any questions. I said no and thanked them all.

I picked up the phone and called Dick. By now it was after midnight. I gave him the worst news imaginable. He was shocked, distraught, and crying. We were both crying. This couldn't be happening. It was surreal. Our son, who we brought into the world, was gone. It was starting to fully register, and I was getting numb.

Terri and I stayed up for a long time, going over the events of the evening. She never left my side. I got an emotional call from John. He said he had to spend the night in jail. He said he was so sorry, stating, "Oh God, I've ruined us." He was crying, choking. I reassured him that it was okay; he didn't ruin us. He told me he loved me so much, and then he had to hang up. Terri and I tried to sleep when it got to be around 3:00 a.m., but neither of us could. I kept hoping it was all a bad dream. Everybody says that when they lose a loved one, and now I knew why.

TRAUMA

In the morning, Terri left to go back to her house. I called to check on James and sat down to compose an e-mail:

> *Dear Friends,*
>
> *With the heaviest of hearts, I give you the news that our son Marshall passed away yesterday. As most of you already know, Marshall suffered with bipolar disorder, a most insidious illness that is all but impossible to treat. Marshall struggled with bipolar since being diagnosed with it in 05 while serving in the navy.*
>
> *We watched as our once joyful, exuberant, considerate, and loving son became tormented and tortured with furious fits of rage and delusional, bizarre behavior. To witness this can only be described as terrifying. I don't understand it and never will.*
>
> *By the grace of God, Marshall has been called home and is now at peace.*
>
> *Thank you for your prayers. We appreciate all your support.*
>
> *Love,*
>
> *John and Shirlee Gentles*

I made a call to Baue Funeral Home to set up an appointment to make funeral arrangements. I knew two of our pastors were out of the country, so left a message for one of the pastor's wives Beth, a friend of mine.

The phone didn't stop ringing. News stations called to interview me; news teams drove down the street, filming our house. A reporter, Robert Patrick from the St. Louis post-dispatch, knocked on the door and introduced himself. "Could I ask you some questions?"

"No!" I told him. "Please leave us alone." Rebecca Wu from News Channel 5 knocked on the door. She asked for a picture of Marshall, stating it was going to be on the news. I gave her a photo of Marshall. Kara Caswell from Channel 4 wanted an interview, as did a reporter named Joel Currier. I told them all, "Please, never call again."

I called my mom, my siblings, our daughters—everyone was in shock, crying.

I got a call from the county jail telling me I could come and pick up my husband and that we'd be contacted by prosecuting attorney Jack Banas's office very soon.

I drove to the jail and took the elevator up to John's floor. He was escorted out of his cell and handed his shoes and belt. I heard the guard tell him sincerely, "Good luck, man." John looked at me, and I could tell he hadn't slept. His eyes were red. He was hesitant to hug me, not sure of his reception. In a hoarse whisper he said, "I love you, and I'm so sorry"

"I know," I said. "It's okay."

When we got home, I picked up James from the neighbor's house. Heather and Allison had flown in from Chicago and were already at the house. We sat on the couch, hugging each other. After awhile, the girls sat on either side of their dad, resting their heads on his shoulders. The trauma was palpable.

The pastor's wife, Beth, came over after listening to my phone message. With her husband out of town, she took it upon herself to offer comfort and prayers. As the acting choir director, she offered to coordinate the music for the funeral service. She enlisted the help of the music director, Greg, and together they made plans. She asked us to come up with Bible verses and memories that would be printed on the bulletin. We were grateful for her kind offer and accepted readily. We agreed to meet in a day or two to go over everything.

That same day, we met with Baue director Don White to make funeral arrangements and select a casket. We were planning the unthinkable, both of us broken. The three kids sorted through photographs to assemble on picture boards. It was good for them to have a project, a distraction, as they wrestled with their grief.

Pastor Keller and Vicar Rob Biesendorfer stopped over at our house to console and pray with us. John was not doing well and would audibly choke back tears. He had his own panic attacks now. When I witnessed him starting to hyperventilate, I called Rob. He'd drop whatever he was doing and come over in a moment. John apologized to him each time, stating that he knew he was on suicide watch. We put an obituary in the paper and on Baue's website and started receiving calls and cards of condolence. Beth and I put the final touches on the bulletin that included Bible verses selected by the girls and us. My family arrived. Dick, Kathy, and her daughter, Amy, drove down from Dundee the night before the funeral and stayed in a nearby hotel.

I had asked a friend from choir, named John, to call Dick as a favor to me. His brother suffers from bipolar and was, therefore, very familiar with the manifestations of the illness. I thought this would help Dick to not only understand Marshall's rapid decline, but to act as a bridge when he arrived, a familiar voice that would welcome him at our end. He graciously did me this favor.

On January 17, Heather's twenty-eighth birthday, an occasion a that should warrant celebration, cake, and gifts, we prepared instead for her brother's funeral.

Overshadowed, by Marshall's death, I knew we'd have to ensure that it was a celebratory occasion in the future. All three kids, Heather, Allison, and James spent most of the day putting together five picture boards that would be displayed at the funeral.

The service on Friday, January 18, was undeniably beautiful. Pastors Paul Schult and Charles Schlie returned from their mission trip from Cambodia the evening prior. They were aware of Marshall's death through e-mail and worked on the eulogy during the thirteen-hour-fight home. I called a couple of Marshall's friends, and soon the word spread. There was such a huge turnout at the funeral home that before the service began we were moved to their largest room to accommodate the crowd. Pastor Schult and Vicar Biesendorfer performed the service with extraordinary emotion, interjecting stories about Marshall and relating their own personal experiences. When Liz started off the service by singing "Amazing Grace," it was sung with such feeling her voice broke a few times. Beth sang "Awesome in This Place," and her voice, too, cracked with emotion. My friend Greg played the keyboard and sang "In Christ Alone," backed by a dozen or more members of the choir. It was a glorious collaboration of friends, family, and church. I didn't see it, but was told that during the third verse of "In Christ Alone" Dick leaned forward and placed his hand on John's shoulder. That explained why Pastor Schult and members of the choir were suddenly overcome with emotion during that particular song.

Heather wrote a tribute to her brother that was printed on the back of the bulletin:

Marshall Robert Fink, born August 11, 1981

Fun-loving son, amazing brother, caring nephew, and good friend. He was an extraordinary man with a humble heart.

Compassionate, warm, and selfless, he put everyone else first.

As kids, Marsh, Alli, and I were the three musketeers. We were the "kiddies," all piling in the backseat of our parents' car for float trips, six flags excursions, zoo visits, Sunday morning Burger King trips, and most of all, our trip to Africa and Out West.

I remember our late night talks we would have after one of us would get home from being out, or sometimes we both would just stay in and have movie nights. We were fiercely protective of each other, especially of our younger siblings, Alli and James.

Although I was the oldest, he in so many ways took care of Alli, James, and me. Marshall always asked how you were doing. He wanted to know about others before himself. A trait he learned from his father, Dick.

Marshall's laugh was contagious. His ability to tell a story brought out his witty, jokester side. It brought out his goofy smile, which he passed onto James. And Marshall gave the warmest hugs. He didn't want to let go.

Marshall joined the navy in September of 2001 to serve his country. He excelled greatly. He found his niche. He loved California, his friends, and his ship. He was so proud to have his family there, to show us around his ship, his bunk.

Marshall developed bipolar disorder in late summer of 2005. Sadly, as much as he tried to fight his illness (God knows he did), he couldn't fight it and succumbed to his illness January 11, 2008. Our family knows that Marshall is at peace in heaven. Alli, James, and I know that he is looking down on us, watching over, guarding, and protecting us. He is our angel. He is our Marshy.

Our funeral procession arrived at Jefferson Barrack's National Cemetery. Final prayers were given by Pastor Schult and Vicar Biesendorfer. It was blistery cold. We watched in revered silence, the "Three Gun Salute," and the ceremonious folding of the flag, which draped Marshall's casket. I knew the flag was important to Dick, and as a final goodwill gesture, I motioned for the guards to give it to him. This was not protocol; the flag was usually presented to the soldier's mother. I reasoned that, being divorced, we were unable to share it. I had someone to come home to, whereas he did not. After a moment of awkwardness, the guard, not trusting my hand gesture, leaned close to hear my verbal cue. That settled, it was presented to Dick with white-gloved hands.

We invited everyone back to our house after the funeral. Dick declined, stating he wasn't ready to see the place where his son breathed his last breath.

A large group of us stayed up late, talking into the wee hours of the morning, never wanting to let go, never wanting to say good-bye to one another. Heather, Alli, Pat, Mom, Jessica, Melissa, Terri, Kathy, Valda, and my brother Alan—all of us reminiscing. Marshall was a treasure to us all.

DISHONORABLE

On January 19, 2008, only one day day after the funeral, Marshall received a letter from:

> *Department of the Navy*
> *Secretary of the Navy Council of Review Boards*
> *720 Kennon ST SE Rm 309 (NDRB)*
> *Washington NYD DC 20374-5023*
> *Notice of Decision That Discharge Is Proper As Issued*
> *The review authority has carefully examined all available official records in connection with your application for discharge review.*
> *The final decision is that the discharge is proper as issued and that no change is warranted.*
> *Enclosure (1) is a copy of the record of review of discharge. The original has been made a part of the official service personnel record.*
> *T.D.Sidbury*
> *Executive Secretary*

I fell to my knees, unable to catch my breath. After all the fighting to get Marshall's status changed to honorable, and now he'd just been declared other than honorable again. The room started spinning; I was sick. He was disgraced. They won't allow him to be buried at Jefferson Barracks now, and I'll have to have his body transferred to a new cemetery. I did not have any more fight left in me. I called my brother in a state of near hysteria. "They're going to dig Marshall back up. He won't be allowed to stay at Jefferson Barracks. He's just been declared other than honorable. How could this be happening?"

Alan said, "No, they wouldn't do that."

"How do you know?" I asked. "I've got the letter right here in my hands!"

I was convinced that the naval council's decision would most certainly supersede that of the regional VA. Then I placed a call to Richard Ivy, and since it was Saturday, I left him a message. I sobbed and sobbed, wracked with tears, all within the privacy of Marshall's bedroom.

Richard Ivy called me back and reassured me, "The VA regional office already made the decision to change your son's status to honorable, and that stands. We overturned it, and it's staying that way!" He continued, "There is no reason to be alarmed. Marshall's AWOL was consistent with his bipolar disease. Only convicted felons must remain other than honorable, *not* him!"

Once again, I wanted to hug this man! I owed him so much!

Then Mr. Ivy made some suggestions:
- Request *entire* C&P (compensation and pension) file to include service *and* medical records (Not merely the C&P dated 02/12/07, but *all* three exams, due to "our son passing away"
- Get information from freedom of information clerk
- Write back to board; his mental illness clears his name!

I thought, *I've got to fight this. I will fight this. Just not now. I'm grieving!*

On January 21, John asked me to accompany him to a new law office. Not wishing to leave his fate to chance, John wanted to consult with an attorney. I thought we should wait and present our case to the prosecuting attorney, reasoning that the evidence spoke for itself. Once there, John thought it was necessary to proceed with his defense. I was not happy to sign the consent, knowing we could ill afford the retainer. No matter, it went on a credit card.

The next few days were spent on auto-pilot. James had returned to school on the twenty-second, and John went back to work that same day. I was summoned to give a statement to the state's prosecuting attorney, Jack Banas. My sister Pat had driven back up to be with me, and on the twenty-third, we headed downtown, armed with documents and the photo boards from the funeral.

We were escorted in and introduced to Mr. Banas and another prosecuting attorney named Kent Fanning. I was prepared to fervently defend John's actions and presented my extensive file on Marshall's previous hospitalizations. They started out by saying they'd done a thorough investigation. They heard the recordings of my phone calls to 911, as well as Marshall's voice before the phone was disconnected. They seemed somewhat apologetic about the rather slow response of the police to arrive at the house. I pointed out that Marshall was very strong and that he'd pinned a doctor to the floor during a hospitalization the Christmas before last and that his rage was out of control the night he died. I showed documents in chronological order going back to when he was first diagnosed with the illness in 05 and how we tried to get Marshall the help he needed. They agreed that the government is lacking on funding for mental health and that it needs to be addressed.

They asked about the dynamics of the relationship between John and Marshall. I was glad I'd brought the picture boards, which reinforced a close, loving relationship going back to when Marshall was four years old. I explained the manifestations of bipolar disorder, and both nodded, having previous knowledge of this.

They had already done their homework, interviewing everyone at Marshall's place of employment. He'd made repeated bizarre calls to his coworkers, which they taped and played back to him that last week. They said that when Marshall heard his own voice on the tapes, he walked out of the room. In one call, Marshall stated that he had "penguins on his feet." How I wished I had called Marshall's coworkers with my growing concerns that week. Apparently, a couple of the guys tried to look me up but having a different last name than my son, were unable to locate me. Mr. Banas and Mr. Fanning agreed that John was only acting in self-defense.

On January 25, the St. Charles County Sheriff's Department received a phone call from prosecuting attorney Kent Fanning. "After meeting with Jack Banas and the mother of the victim, they reviewed the case and feel that John Gentles acted in self-defense when he fatally shot Marshall Fink on Friday." January 11, 2008. Kent stated that "they are not going to file charges in this case and the case should now be considered *closed*."

Later that day, I was looking through Marshall's things, and in his bottom dresser drawer I found the empty Dimetapp bottle I'd recently purchased for James's cold. It was lying next to three empty liquor bottles. I found what I thought was an empty box in his closet. But when I peered inside, I discovered where he'd been stashing all his meds since he stopped taking them.

While cleaning out Marshall's car the next day, I turned on the engine to remove the CDs. Loaded into the disc player was an album by the horror punk group The

Misfits, the 1982 release *Walk Among Us* (live version). The manically repeated lyrics of the song that blared was, "Mommy, can I go out and kill tonight." Other discs: Marilyn Manson's violent "Holy Wood," and again The Misfits with "Static Age."

My first day back to work was January 28, 2008. I felt so out of place there now. I had my own spa room that was beautifully appointed contemporary and Zen. The dim lighting and tranquil meditation CDs had always been so soothing in the past. Now, I found it to be too melancholy. It was a struggle to get through a facial without losing my composure.

I had an appointment with an attorney that same day to start proceedings to settle Marshall's small estate.

Life was in slow motion. John and I said a lot more I love yous, but these were spoken solemnly.

My grief was gaining a stronghold on me now while writing thank-you notes. To Dick I wrote:

Dearest Dick, 2/11/08
I'm so sad that we lost our precious Marshall. No one feels the depth of this more than you and me. The comfort I receive is in knowing Marshall is now with his heavenly Father. I listen to the memorial CD as Pastor Schult's words are comforting. I play it every day in my car. Someday soon I will gather photos of Marshall's life and send them to you. Marshall's headstone will be finished and in place by next week. When you are ready, I'd like you to come and visit. You can sort through Marshall's belongings, and we can go to the cemetery. Each day on this earth is truly a gift from God so we must respect that. Someday soon

enough we'll be reunited with our beloved son in heaven and will rejoice forever.
Love,
Shirlee

One reporter in particular, Joel Currier, was persistent in trying to get an interview. I turned him down consistently, resenting his intrusion. Then my mother called to say that a reporter wanted to do a story on her grandson, and she let him in the house, showing him photos of Marshall. I said, "Oh no, Mom. I wish you hadn't talked to him." I called this reporter to give him accurate information, because he stated that he'd print the story anyway, based on what he'd heard from my mother.

I sent out an e-mail to friends that read:

Greetings,

I'm writing to let you know that there will be an article appearing in the Post-Dispatch either Sunday or Monday about Marshall and our family. I had previously turned down the journalist's (Joel Currier) request for an interview on three separate occasions. However, I learned that he'd already spoken to a few family members, including charming my mother into inviting him into her home. Mr. Currier made it clear in his numerous messages that he would be printing the story with or without my input. Uncertain of his motives and fearing exploitation of our grief, I wanted to make it clear that I did not initiate or solicit this attention.

Thank You,
Shirlee Gentles

It just so happens that after meeting Mr. Currier, I liked the guy. Maybe initially he had hoped for something salacious, like me implicating John perhaps. But the more I talked to him, his compassion was palpable, and he was only interested in relating the facts, which did not need embellishment. Joel stated that, "His story will touch the lives of many families struggling with mental illness." We spoke or e-mailed regularly, with him giving me projected dates for the article. Tragically, there was a shooting at the Kirkwood City Hall that pre-empted and dominated the papers for well over a week.

A cousin of mine from Nevada was stunned when he heard about Marshall and asked my brother Mike about the tragedy. He'd corresponded regularly with Mike via e-mail and didn't want to upset me by asking. My brother wrote the following intuitive letter dated February 18, 2008:

> Hi, Robert,
> Well, I'm a bit uncomfortable with this. It is better to let Shirlee communicate with you, when and if she is ready. But she and John are also struggling, I'm sure, to get their lives back to normal. And I want to support them rather than spread whatever incomplete information I have. I'm sending this also to Shirlee—hope I'm not out-of-line, Shirl.
> I last saw Marshall on his birthday, August 11th, of last year. On his medication, he was his same old self. I really liked him, far beyond just because he was my nephew, and I still can't think about him without becoming very depressed.
> With his family, he visited me in Africa. I was amazed at how readily he fit in in such a foreign environment. He was such a relaxed, easygoing guy. While we were buying trinkets at a market,

a Swazi asked him for a cigarette, and I watched while they spent quite awhile carrying on a conversation.

I think his growing interest in foreign lands is partially what propelled him to the navy.
He did very well in the navy, and then, inexplicably, something went wrong. Drugs? Claustrophobia on ship? Stress? Wrong for me to speculate. But it resulted in his lashing out at superiors and discharge, followed by his disappearance for several months. The navy was his whole life. Shirlee didn't know if he was dead or alive but eventually tracked him down at a broken down hotel in Yuma. After a long time, she convinced him to come home, forced him onto medication, wrote numerous letters to the navy to get him changed to honorable discharge with full medical benefits, and her and John welcomed him into their home while he got reestablished,

even though we often talked on the phone in hushed tones, and they were often scared of him. I'd really rather not dwell on incidents I was told about. I'm sure neither would Shirlee and John. The funeral was all about a celebration of his life. You know, he wasn't "broken" before he entered the navy, and he entered soon after 9/11 out of a surging feeling of patriotism.

So he had a second chance at life. He got a job as a marine mechanic and did very well, saving money for a house, etc. When I saw him, he let me take his monster motorbike for a spin and offered for me to also try his mini-bikes. He had such a calm and unassuming manner and was happy if you were happy. We talked while he loaded his bike onto his truck, heading out for a weekend of dirt-biking fun and camping with his buddies.

I don't know… I don't like to read anything into this, but there seemed to also be a note of sadness in his demeanor, a hesitation to leave. Perhaps a fear that someone would bring up the subject of his illness, maybe a desire for all his problems to just disappear into the same calm that so often typified him. I never saw him during any of his episodes. I'm really glad I didn't.

A facet, it seems, of this illness is a belief, while on medication, that you are okay—that you are no longer sick, that you don't need the meds. Marshall went off his meds with a dramatic and instant effect. What I understand is that he made some nonsense calls to his buddies. When asked about these calls, he denied making them. They played back a tape of them, and he turned around and walked out. Too embarrassed to go back to work and unwilling to resume his meds, he reverted back to his sickness, culminating in his attack on his mother and brother and stepfather and his tragic death.

That's about it. Marshall was buried at a naval cemetery outside of St. Louis with full honors. There will be a long article on Marshall appearing sometime soon in the St. Louis Post-Dispatch. I'm looking forward to reading it. As per Shirlee's inputs, it will be more about his life than his death.

Stay well and stay happy, Mike

On February 26, 2008, the following article did appear on the front page of the *Post-Dispatch*.

Bipolar Disorder Shatters Family, Ends in Death
By Joel Currier

The veins in Marshall Fink's neck bulged with fury as he pumped his fist, telling his parents they should stick a shotgun in their mouths and pull the trigger.

His mother and stepfather begged Fink, 26, to take his medication and calm down. That set him off.

Fink put his fingers to his head, pretending to have a gun, then pointed at his parents. He chest-bumped his mother into the garage, snarling and telling her she should die.

Shirlee and John Gentles called 911 several times the night of January 11th.

The police were on their way, but by the time they arrived, John Gentles had fatally shot his stepson.

In a little over two years, Fink's satisfying career in the navy dissolved into a struggle with bipolar disorder that tormented him and ripped apart his family. His psychiatrist says the stress of the navy career he loved contributed to the disease.

Chaotic Night

"Please, Marshall, you're hurting me, and I love you," said Shirlee Gentles, 52. "You're scaring me, and I just want you to get help."

She ran outside to the driveway. But Fink dragged her back inside. He had punched holes in the garage drywall. "You're not going anywhere," he yelled.

Gentles grabbed her twelve-year-old son, James, and managed to run to a neighbor's house.

Meanwhile, her husband took his 9mm pistol out of the closet and showed it to his stepson, who did not have a weapon.

"Marshall, this is loaded, and you're going to listen to us," said Gentles, 62. "You need to go to the hospital."

Fink lunged and got within an arm's length of his stepfather when Gentles fired one shot into Fink's stomach. He bled to death on the kitchen floor.

Police arrested Gentles, a dentist, questioned him, and released him the next day.

Prosecutors said he killed Fink in self-defense, and no charges were filed.

A Happy Childhood

Shirlee Gentles remarried and moved to the St. Louis area when Fink was five years old. He grew up with two stepsisters, Heather, now 28, and Allison, now 23, and his half-brother, James.

Fink's family said he and his stepfather had a good relationship but that Fink was closer to his father, Richard "Dick" Fink, who lived near Chicago. Together they restored classic cars and motorcycles and spent many weekends attending swap meets and auto shows.

"He was just fantastic about cars," said Heather Gentles. "He and Dick shared that passion."

Jonathan Coffin, one of Fink's best friends in high school, said they often stayed up all night restoring Fink's light blue, rare Mustang and cruising.

Coffin, 26, of St. Peters, also said Fink was a talented guitarist who loved jamming to his favorite songs by the Doors, Metallica, and the Grateful Dead.

Fifteen months after graduation from Francis Howell High School, Fink enlisted in the navy, inspired by the September 11th attacks to serve his country.

Illness Takes Hold

Fink was stationed at the naval base in San Diego as a mechanic aboard the *Peleliu* assault ship.

"It was a natural fit that he would go and work on engines," Shirlee Gentles said.

For more than three years, his service record was clean; his superiors even wrote him several letters of commendation. Fink wanted a career in the navy, but a conflict of highs and lows was escalating inside his head.

"Something happened to him in the navy," Heather Gentles said. "He just was never going to be the same."

"Fink's illness developed quickly and was brought on in part by stress and lack of sleep," said his psychiatrist in St. Charles, Dr. Greg Mattingly. "Fink's condition emerged about the same age as most bipolar patients," Mattingly said, "and was not spurred by any specific traumatic incident."

"With bipolar, you can go from pretty much normal one day, to the next day being very, very, very sick," Mattingly said.

Fink mouthed off to his commanders, stopped eating regularly, and lost twenty pounds. He grew increasingly paranoid, and in September 2005, doctors at the Naval Medical Center in San Diego diagnosed his condition as bipolar disorder, which often results in episodes of severe depression and in mania. It affects more than 5 million Americans.

"Most people who develop the disorder are genetically predisposed to it," Mattingly said. "Along with stress and sleep deprivation," he said, "substance abuse is another common trigger. Fink had begun taking legal stimulants as part of a body-building regimen."

Because of Fink's diagnosis, the navy started discharge proceedings. Fink challenged the diagnosis. He wanted the chance to return to active duty, but the navy considered him unfit to serve.

Devastated, Fink went AWOL, hoping it would somehow delay his discharge.

Fink made plans to come home for Christmas. His mother drove to the airport on Christmas Day, but he hadn't boarded his flight. Meanwhile, the navy declared Fink a deserter.

His mother looked for him for almost two months. She made dozens of phone calls to navy commanders, comrades, and congressmen seeking their help.

Thinking her son could have been kidnapped or killed, she called the police in San Diego to report him missing.

Detectives checked bank records and found an ATM transaction in Yuma, Arizona, where police tracked him to a motel.

Officers returned him to base to face a trial by court martial. Fink accepted a discharge classified as "other than honorable" in lieu of a trial. His mother is still fighting to have his discharge changed to honorable.

Back to St. Charles County

In September 2006, Fink packed up a U-Haul and drove from San Diego to Weldon Spring in two days, hardly stopping.

As soon as he got home, he closed all the window blinds because he believed people were watching him.

Fink became a night owl. He rarely slept. He paced at night and slammed doors when he'd go outside to smoke. Once, at 2:00 a.m., he grabbed a pitchfork and began turning mulch in the yard.

Fink stopped eating because he thought his parents were trying to poison him. Instead of food, he took ephedrine pills, caffeine powder, and drank his parent's liquor. He hid the empty bottles in his room, where he spent hours sitting alone in the dark.

"When I came home last year, something was off. It just wasn't him," his stepsister said. "Somehow, Marshall was locked away."

Fink became delusional. He thought Nazis were coming after him and talked of holding down his little brother to give him a tattoo of a swastika because he thought he was a Nazi.

Shirlee Gentles says she saw more than a dozen doctors to treat her own medical problems caused by anxiety over her son.

The loaded revolver she found under her son's bed pillows compounded her fears.

"Every night for almost two years, I slept with one eye open because I thought he was going to kill me."

Getting Help

Three months after he came home, his parents had him committed to St. Joseph Health Center in St. Charles, where he was put on suicide watch. During treatment, Fink attacked a doctor and was put in restraints.

After almost a month, he felt well enough to come home, thanks to new medication.

Fink found a job as a mechanic at a boat dealership and repair shop in St. Charles. His coworkers said he was funny, polite, and reliable.

Fink even wanted to buy a house and took his grandmother, Hazel Nyquist, with him to look at homes for sale in St. Louis.

"Just the week before (the shooting), I was saying, 'It's a good thing Marshall's feeling so good,'" said Nyquist, 86 of St. Peters. "I thought things were really moving along. Apparently, they weren't."

In the weeks before his death, Fink confided in a coworker that he felt lonely and depressed.

Meanwhile, the family struggled to help Fink get better. This past Christmas, Fink attended a family gathering in the Chicago area where he saw his father.

"It was a real joy to have him be with us," said Richard Fink, 56, of Dundee, Illinois. "He seemed good."

But he said his son complained of frequent headaches brought on by medication. So Fink stopped taking it.

The Final Days

Fink further isolated himself in the last days of his life. He stayed in his room most of the time. He called in sick to work. On days he did work, his coworkers said he was distracted, spending at least ten hours on tasks that should have taken two hours.

At one point, Fink called his stepfather to the computer to show him a video on the Internet of an execution-style killing.

Shirlee and John Gentles suspected he had stopped taking his medication, and his mother began arrangements to have him committed again.

On the night of his death, Shirlee Gentles said Fink was tormented by anger she had never seen. "There's no way to explain what happened that day," she said.

Fink's father has questioned the shooting, wondering why John Gentles grabbed his gun instead of leaving the house to wait for police to arrive.

"If he didn't have this weapon, what would have happened? A black eye?" Richard Fink said.

When police told Gentles that Fink had died, he gasped and buried his face in his hands.

"I didn't want to kill him," Gentles told detectives. I just wanted to stop him because I thought he was going to kill us."

Shirlee Gentles said her husband is still too distraught to discuss with anyone the night he killed his stepson.

Finding Peace

The Gentleses' home is calm again. There is no more pacing in the dark. No more slamming doors. No more screaming.

And for the first time in more than two years, Shirlee Gentles says she can sleep through the night without worrying.

She doesn't blame her husband for killing their son. She blames the disorder for destroying the person he used to be.

"This illness robbed us of a beautiful, beautiful son," she says. "On the one hand, I would do anything to have him back. On the other, we have peace of mind."

We received an outpouring of letters from strangers, people who'd read the article on Marshall and felt compelled to write. Most letters were channeled through Mr. Currier who then forwarded them on to us.

1. "Thanks for the Marshall Fink story. This story encourages a lot of families at different levels of living through mental distress. We are not in this alone."
2. "Well written, a tough topic, and a tragic, misunderstood illness."
3. "Nice job on today's story about Marshall Fink and his family. Very compelling."
4. "Joel, your story explains the Achilles heel of current psychiatric practice under which the patient is responsible for his

own treatment (taking meds), yet the patient's condition (brain disorder) makes it difficult or impossible to be responsible for his own care. Our system is broken. Please believe it."

5. " I actually can't recall the last time I read an article written by a *Post-Dispatch* reporter that I thought was Pulitzer Prize quality reporting and editing, but the article in today's newspaper struck me as worthy of such an accolade. I want to thank the reporter and the editor of the story for presenting the tragedy with such compassion and attention to the details regarding the illness and its effect on families."

6. "This is a topic with a lot of visibility lately as the *New York Times* has run many segments. My daughter has a mood disorder. These types of conditions are all brain health issues that present themselves across a variety of symptoms. At least a broken arm is a broken arm. A spectrum brain illness is a moving target that changes in impact and intensity. Many are faced with a big challenge and are succeeding by advocating greater awareness and education. Mainly, it's a daily struggle where stereotypes hold fast so we do not have to pay for alternatives. Thanks again for the story."

7. "Your story today was very moving on a personal level. My daughter is bipolar. After a two-year period of blessed peace

wherein she was fully medication compliant, she went off her meds last summer and has declined steadily and rapidly. She has been hospitalized three times in the last six months; in fact, she was just released from a ten-day hospitalization. Unfortunately, she refused meds for the first week of her stay. She is currently back on her meds, but I've learned not to get my hopes up. She never has the depressive episodes, just pure manic (maybe unipolar would be a better diagnosis?), and her manic phases are pure rage. She has also been diagnosed with a borderline personality disorder. The hallmark of BPD is anger—she could be their poster child. Anyway, thanks for writing about the subject in a way that explains what a terrible disease this is—you do mourn the child that was."

8. "This story is a sad testament to the state of mental health care in St. Louis, and I imagine the rest of the country as well. Comparing a phone book from five years ago with one today, one would see a tremendous drop in the number of treatment facilities available to people with mental illness and/or chemical dependencies. There are even fewer inpatient facilities, and those with inpatient care often have the thirty days and you are "miraculously" cured and let go plan, which basically translates to "that's as much as the insurance company will pay for." Getting

treatment for someone with bipolar or schizophrenia is nearly impossible, given the fact that they are paranoid and suspicious of the treatment. There is no way to force them to seek treatment unless they are considered "a danger to themselves or others." What is the standard of proof that a mentally ill person is dangerous? Making threats to kill someone or oneself does not meet the standard of proof. Even attempting suicide does not. So it seems that unless someone has actually carried out a threat are they then qualified for mandatory treatment. Obviously, by that point it is too late. Therefore, do not blame the illness for the tragic consequences. These disorders are treatable and manageable. Were there more access to treatment we might have avoided situations such as this, the Kirkwood City Hall massacre, and the recent school shootings in Northern Illinois and Virginia Tech."

Four letters were addressed to us:

Dear Mr. and Mrs. Gentles, February 28th,

I read with great interest the article in the Post-Dispatch about the tragedy involving your son, Marshall. I then took a chance on getting your address through Google search. I hope you will not consider this an intrusion into your private family life by a total stranger.

I am a USAF Catholic chaplain, presently serving at Osan AB in South Korea. My home of record is Belleville, Illinois, right across the river from you, and one of my daily habits is to read several newspapers throughout the US, including the St. Louis Post. The article caught my eye because my family as well was deeply affected by the bipolar disorder in my oldest brother who suffered its ravages for forty-three years until his death in 2003. I do not want to go into the details of my story for fear of being misinterpreted as playing the suffering Olympics game—my suffering is worse than your suffering sort of thing. You know what I'm talking about, and you don't need anything more to add to your grief.

The unspeakable pain of Marshall's illness that led to his death should be obvious to anyone who read the article, but for those of us who have been where you are, your words describe precisely the hopelessness, the grief, and the anxiety that mental illness causes in a family. That wonderful picture in the paper when times were better is striking testimony of the devastation mental illness brings to anyone within the range of love. I think of the hope, the promise, the dreams you once felt that his young life offered as he was growing up through the years of care and nurturing, and I weep for him and for you. I know how upside down your life has been; I know how desperately Marshall did not want to be mentally ill, and I know how much you wanted life to be good to him. It simply could not be that way. I hope you have enough family and friends to throw their arms around you to share the depth of their love and sorrow.

I write to lend you support, understanding, and most profound expressions of sympathy. The torture and torment are over for Marshall, and now nothing or no one can ever hurt him again. I realize that may be little consolation for you who want him back whole and healed, but maybe this is the only way he could ever again have any peace.
As you continue to mourn the loss of your son, may you find comfort and hope in the days ahead.
God's grace and peace,
David V. USAF
Catholic Chaplain
Osan AB Korea

Dear Mr. and Mrs. Gentles,
I read with great interest the article in the Post-Dispatch, and first I would like to express my deepest sympathy in the loss of your son.
I definitely feel your pain as I have a twenty-nine-year-old son that is bipolar schizophrenic.
I was a widow for seven years before I remarried. He made my husband's life hell. I tried to seek treatment and help for him, but because of his age, eighteen at the time, I could not force him to take his medication or go for treatment. I felt that the system and the mental health specialists were of no help. I lived in Cleveland, Ohio, at the time, and they were forever cutting back on mental health funding. I later found out that mental health funds were being cut nationwide.
I have written to all of the presidential hopefuls and inquired as to why everyone is concentrating

on medical care and not mental health care and treatment.

There were times that I wished my son was dead along with myself because of the stress his actions put me through.

My husband was from this area, and after his retirement he decided to move back, to get away from my son, which is why I am here.

However, I am glad to say that my son, since my departure, is now taking his medications and trying to become a productive member of society. So I don't feel as bad about leaving him.

Again, I want to express my sympathy and encourage you both to get on with your life. Though it's tragic, it is not your fault.

May God bless and keep you both in his loving arms.

Sincerely,

T. P.

Dr. and Mrs. Gentles, 3/17/08

In January when I read about the terrible event in your lives, my thoughts and prayers were with all of you. My husband and I were grateful that no charges were filed.

When the article appeared in the Post-Dispatch on 2/26/08, I shed many tears for you. Perhaps I was shedding those tears for myself!

We, too, have a very intelligent, twenty-nine-year-old son who could not complete his last semester of college due to the horrible disorder of bipolar disease. My husband and I could have written the article and changed the names, and *it would have been appropriate for us, except for the sad ending.*

My son has had many hospitalizations. He has been on every medication available. We were on a first-name basis with the Manchester Police Department. He currently is residing in a group home in Jefferson County. His future life has been ruined as a result of legal and financial issues, which compound his mental health issues.

Until someone lives with a child they love and cherish, they cannot know the pain, fear, and suffering that parents and the family experience. We slept with our bedroom door blocked by exercise equipment. We slept with a gun in an easily accessible location. You've been there! You know! We just want you to know that we've been there. We share your pain and God forbid, could be there again.

The final paragraph in the 2/26/08 article could not have been more appropriate. May you continue to have peace.

Sincerely,
P. R.

Dear Shirlee,
I think that you must be the most courageous woman to have printed the story of your son's death for the newspaper. I say this because it gives people who do not have any idea what it is like to deal with mentally handicapped loved ones. You also made it more clear about our dear military who have left the service and have such needs, which are delayed or not attended to at all.

I thoroughly understand bipolar since my dear aunt and some of her six children had it. One of my female cousins committed suicide in her early sixties a couple years ago.

They gave my aunt so many shock treatments that her retinas detached in both eyes, until my uncle said no more. Then they discovered what she had all along—bipolar. I know others with the same situation. They describe it this way: hell on earth until properly diagnosed. You have been so brave to come to church right away with your family, and now you are singing again with the Praise Team. I know how terribly hard it must be for your husband, and I pray that he is getting help for that. In fact, I laud your whole family for setting a great example for all of us, knowing that there is a big hole in each heart.

I just wanted to tell you how I felt and thank you for your article. It helped all of us to understand the situation better.

God's blessings and peace be to you and John and your children.

Love in Christ,
C. A.

We received a lovely letter from an old girlfriend of Marshall's:

Dear Shirlee,

I am deeply sad for your loss. I probably haven't seen Marshall since high school, but he was an awesome person to be around. The picture I enclosed was the last day of our eighth grade year.

I will always remember him and the great memories of us having fun with JC, Matt, and Dustin! With all my love,
Maggie C.

BLAME

On March 6, Heather and Alli ran in the half marathon; the back of their T-shirts imprinted with Marshall's name. They didn't run for glory or to win. They ran in his memory, stopping along the way to reflect on the life they once shared with their brother.

On the eleventh of March, I had a dream that I was walking past Marshall's bedroom. I saw a form under his covers then his hands peeked out from the covers. I was standing next to his bed now, closely examining his hands, and they were detailed and *perfect*! I realize that he is not dead after all. I thought, *How could they have made such a horrific mistake when, clearly, these are his real hands?* Then his head comes into view, and now I know for certain that, thank God, he's still alive. But when I go to hug him, he lunges at me. Frightened, I say, "Marshall, I only want to hug you!" He just glares at me in anger.

Life gradually got back to a more normal rhythm. I called Dick on occasion and told him the door was open whenever he felt that he was ready. He said the same thing. "Not ready now. I'll let you know." I had resumed choir and was in preparation for the musical *Let All Heaven Rejoice*. Heather visited James's school on Special Person's Day, something she did every year. James had his head shaved on St. Baldrick's Day. And on March 15th, I took James to Lutheran High School for his participation in a math contest. I hung around to wait for him and busied myself by reading all the notes that were posted on the bulletin board. I froze when I read the following quote:

The Gun goes off

> And everything
> changes…the world
> changes…and
> Nothing else really matters
> Author Unknown

I went out to my car and buried my face in my hands.

Because of the frozen ground, Marshall's grave and headstone weren't in place until April 16, 2008. When I was notified, I visited the grave that day. I lay my head on the cool marble and sang:

> and I will know though soft ye tread above me
> and then my grave will richer, sweeter be
> and you'll bend down and tell me that you love me
> and I will rest in peace until you come to me

On April 22, 2008, I sent a photo of Marshall's headstone to a few people. His headstone read:

- Marshall Robert Fink
- EN2 USN
- PG IR
- AUG 11, 1981
- JAN 11, 2008
- God Called Him Home Our Beloved Son and Brother

I received a letter from one of Marshall's coworkers, Dan Cross:

> Shirlee, thanks for the photos. My dad is buried there. Not long after Marshall had passed, I went out there to visit them. I know what you mean about the grass. That particular time it had been raining most of the week, and the construction workers were there putting vaults in the ground. I asked this one rather elderly and weathered man if he could help me find Marshall's plot. He said, "Follow me," and away we went. This man was on a mission. I noticed a plywood covered trail, but that, as I would soon find out, was the long way around. He knew a shortcut, and not to be outdone, I accepted the challenge. As I stood there with Marshall, I looked down at my huge mud-caked shoes and had to laugh. Laugh because I knew that Marshall was laughing with me.

We received a letter addressed to John from Dick's lawyer. John was at work and curiosity got the better of me. The letter read:

> Re: Marshall Robert Fink
> *Dear Mr. Gentles,*
> *Please be advised that my firm has been retained by Richard F. Fink to pursue a civil claim for damages arising from the wrongful death of his son, Marshall.*
> *Please have the appropriate representative of your homeowner's insurance contact my office at his or her convenience.*
> *Very Truly Yours,*
> *Attorney__*

A knife sliced through my heart, ripping me in two. I felt there could be no greater injustice in the entire world. I was reeling. I called Dick immediately, and when he answered, I spewed, "*How* could you sue us? Where were *you* when I needed you? What were you thinking?"

He spat back, "Four months...four months, I waited four months and never heard from John."

I said, "What are you talking about? I call you every few weeks inviting you to come here. You keep telling me you're not ready yet, and *we've* been waiting to hear from *you*!"

He said, "It's too late now. John still has a son—James! I have nothing." He spat out John and James names with mocked hatred.

I said, "Dick, this is crazy. You have to know that Marshall would *hate* this, the two people Marshall loved more than anyone in the world fighting one another in court."

He came back with, "Well, you're used to a certain lifestyle, and I want to hurt you the way you hurt me. This is the only way I can do it. I want John to feel my pain, even if the only way I can do it is through his wallet."

I said, "Let me have John call you and talk to you."

Dick said, "No, it's too late for that now. I'm going ahead with the lawsuit, and that's final."

I was actually on my knees now. I felt completely, utterly betrayed—outraged.

All this time I'd been waiting for Dick to come around, waiting for him to come down to hear from John firsthand the events that unfolded the night of Marshall's death. I was convinced that Dick just needed his space initially but eventually would want to hear some of the details regarding Marshall's decline that week. "Dick," I said, "we extended an invitation to you. We've been waiting for *you*!" He said, "I *need* to do this to vindicate Marshall's death, and my attorney agrees with me. My attorney lost a child himself so he knows how I feel." He continued, "I sent for the police report, and I read it thoroughly."

I said, "Well, if that's the case, then you must know that John acted in self-defense."

He said, "No, I don't understand, and why did you have loaded guns lying around the house?"

I said, "Where on earth did you get that idea? We most certainly do *not* have loaded guns lying around. They're in a locked closet, and the bullets are stored separately!"

He said, "It doesn't matter. John took away the only thing I loved, the *only* thing that mattered to me. I'm jealous of John and James and their relationship."

I hung up with Dick and called his sister Kathy. Incredulous, I asked if she knew that Dick was taking action against us. She matter-of-factly said, "Yes, uh-huh."

I asked, "Why didn't you try and talk him out of it?"

She came back with, "Dick already has his mind made up."

I said, "Yes, but do you agree with him? Do you think we are to blame for Marshall's death?"

"Well, we just don't understand, that's all."

"What don't you understand, Kathy?" I asked.

"Why you had guns lying around your house," she said.

"Why on earth would you say something like that, Kathy? Dick said that he read the police report so he must know that's not true. Didn't you read about my calls to 911? You came to our house after the funeral, and you didn't seem upset with us then! What has changed since the last time we spoke?"

She countered with, "Well, Marshall was never violent before, so we don't understand how he could have been violent that night."

Getting more upset by the second, I stated, "Kathy, I've gone over this with you. Marshall was going downhill fast. He stopped taking his meds; he stopped eating; he was drinking heavily every night; he told me to "Get expletive and die." And when I called you to ask how he was acting over Christmas, you stated to me that he was 'Very quiet... very quiet, that's all.' You and Dick both agreed that Marsh was acting very strangely and did not eat anything or converse with you," I said. Getting louder now, I said, "You and your brother never sought help for Marsh. It all rested on my shoulders. And now you're both conspiring to sue us and blame us for his death? This is unbelievable."

She told me not to talk to her this way. She told me she didn't have to listen to me anymore. I said, "Kathy, I considered you my friend, my sister, all these years. Marshall loved us both."

She stated, "Well, Dick's mind is made up, and I'm not going to try and change it." She hung up on me, and we never spoke again.

GUILT, DENIAL

I drove to the county sheriff's department and obtained a copy of the police report. Not sure if I could read it, I decided I must see for myself what Dick misinterpreted as negligence on our part.

1/11/2008

21:03 Ref. to caller's son Marshall Fink - 26 y.o. is bipolar and not taking his medications. Caller was talking very quietly didn't want the son to hear her calling. Phone disconnected. Operator could hear the mother yell at the son before it disconnected.

21:07 Mother wants the son committed to St. Josephs in St. Charles city. Attempted call back. Received answering machine.

21:07 Answering machine again.

21:10 Still getting answering machine, while speaking with female she adv. that she was upstairs.

21:14 Now talking to John Gentles, father, stating that he shot Marshall with a 9mm.

21:14 Rec'd call from mother who said she left house and heard gunshot.

21:14 She is at 52 W Meath Ring

21:14 Father adv that the son is on the floor in the kitchen. Subject is not breathing.

21:15 Son is shot in the abdomen. Male is putting gun in the drawer.

21:16 Road blocked off at the entrance of subdivision, awaiting other units.

21:16 Mother is advised to remain at 52 W Meath Ring.

21:17 Subject is still not moving. John adv. that the son was being aggressive and warned the son before shooting him.

21:23 Have ambulance respond.

21:23 Rec'd call from Shirley Gentles (mom) who adv. she is at 52 Meath Ring and wants disposition as soon as possible.

We (police) arrived and made entry in residence through the open two car garage door. We noticed large holes in the drywall near the door into the home where it appeared someone had punched the wall several times. We entered the home through the garage entry door and discovered Fink lying face down on the kitchen floor. He was not moving. His feet were pointing towards the computer desk, his face was looking away from us, and the top of his head was towards the refrigerator. His left shoulder and upper arm were resting against the base of the kitchen island, his right arm was outstretched pointing towards the sink. Sgt. O immediately checked for respiration and a pulse, however it appeared Fink had neither. At that time we immediately requested medical personnel to respond to provide medical attention. Medic #7 responded, rolled Fink onto his back and attempted to provide medical care, however they declared Fink deceased at 2130 hours.

The remainder of the police report went on to give an interview with John in which he detailed the chain of events of that evening, mirroring my own account. It further read that:

Mr. Gentles stated that he went downstairs and unlocked the gun closet underneath the stairs. He felt he needed to get something after witnessing Marshall pushing Shirlee and punching holes in the drywall. He stated the Marshall was yelling expletives and told them to die. He said he told Marshal that he needed to calm down, that he could not act this way and that he needed to take his medications. Mr. Gentles said that Marshall began to move towards him with a look of RAGE. Mr. Gentles said that Marshall was charging at him with his fists clenched in the air, his face squeezed tight and he could see the veins in his neck bulging. Mr. Gentles said that at that point he was in fear of his life and his families' life. Marshall kept charging at him and Marshall got about one foot away and Mr. Gentles raised the gun and pointed it at his abdomen and fired one shot.

The bluntness of these police documents, with their indifferent description of my son's lifeless body, sickened me, horrified me to be more accurate. And nowhere did it describe the unsafe storage of guns, only that John retrieved a gun from a locked closet.

Heather called on May second, and I told her about the letter we received from Dick's lawyer. She was so saddened. She had spoken to Dick numerous times over the years and had even talked to him a couple of times since Marshall's death.

When John got home from work, he wrote an email to Dick:

> Dick,
> Please let me apologize for not talking to you earlier, especially at the funeral. I have no excuse. I am truly sorry for what happened. For eighteen months, at least, we lived in fear of what might happen if Marshall quit taking his medicine again as he did in December 2006.
> The Marshall our two families knew and loved and admired was not the Marshall on that Friday night.
> As painful as it might be for you to know, Shirlee, James, and I were in fear of our lives that Friday night. Marshall quit taking his medicine earlier that week and continued to drink heavily every night. His psychiatrist said it would only take a few days for him to be paranoid if he quit taking his medicine and made worse if he was drinking. On Friday, Marshall repeatedly threatened us, including telling us to die then telling us how.
> He prevented Shirlee from calling 911 then pulled Shirlee back into the garage. He slammed his fists through the drywall with such force that he broke the second wall on the other side of the studs.
> Then he pushed us back into the house from the garage. During this entire ordeal I did not know where James was. My entire focus was on saving my family.
> When Marshall ran at me, his hands in fists, his muscles bulging, his face red and enraged, I fired only when he was on top of me.

Again, I apologize for not talking to you sooner. I would like to talk to you face-to-face. If you come down to visit Marshall's grave, maybe we can talk then.
John

And then it dawned on me. Dick had never offered condolence or comforting words to me of any sort. I figured he was just so filled with his own grief that he was incapable of offering any to me. I naively envisioned us grieving together at Jefferson Barrack's. I knew he appreciated the gesture when I gave him Marshall's flag. And a couple months after the funeral, my brother Alan handmade a triangular display case for the flag and shipped it to Dick. He was very appreciative and called Alan to thank him. But never once had Dick acknowledged our loss, only his loss.

Heather e-mailed me that evening:

Hi, Shirl,
You know some days it takes every ounce of me to get up. I lie in bed sometimes and just...want to lie. I don't want to get up. I want to lie there and get back in that dream again, that dream where I get to touch and hold Marshall. It's awful waking up and realizing his picture is all I have.
I know how Dick feels—to an extent. No, I don't know what it's like to lose a child—to give birth and raise a son and then lose him unfairly to an illness. I do know what it's like to lose a brother, to feel so responsible, to feel helpless, to feel like I caused all of this. I should have been there, I tell myself. I should be living in St. Louis. I spent time with Marsh in December, and I remember seeing his face, glancing at his face, and think-

ing, He looks sad. But I didn't think anything of it. I didn't think that, my God, he would be so enraged as to lose his life to his illness. I never thought the illness would take him—I at least hoped.

I cannot write thank-you cards. I cry a lot. It hurts. Alli cries, too. I hurt more than Jack knows, more than my family knows. We both are at such a loss. Yet, I feel so much more responsible. I could have stopped all of this if only I was there. I could have been there...

I feel so responsible now for James. I want to hold him every time I see him. Moreover, I try to talk with Dad, and he is standoffish. I know he is grieving. I know he is hurting right now, and that makes me even sadder. I feel like I can't help anyone. Even you, Shirl, I want to wrap my arms around you and make all of this go away. I want you to have peace, you and Dick.

No, it's not fair Marshall got sick. No, life isn't fair and for it to happen to the most beautiful boy in the world. It wasn't fair when my friend Laura was hit by a dump truck. It hurts my heart to think about her, too. She and I were good friends. I still haven't figured out why God takes the best, most kind and loving people. I didn't get to say good-bye to either of them.

I do know that, if anything, God I guess, needed them for something. It better be a good reason to take Marsh and Laura away, you know? I have to tell myself that.

My hope is that Dick can find peace without having to go through this lawsuit ordeal. It brings up

Marshall's death all over again. No, I will never forget my brother, but I certainly do not want him to be remembered for his death but for his life—for his love, his hugs, his everything. When I called Dick today, I wanted to explain that to him, but I feel it isn't the time to say that. I hope I get the chance. I hope that I can remind him who Marshall was and what he wanted. Certainly he didn't want pain for anyone, especially his parents.

I love you,
Heather

I went to work that next day, Friday, and just sat in my car, sobbing. I couldn't get my emotions under control. My boss's wife pulled up alongside my car, and I was crying so hard that I could not talk. She said, "Shirlee, why don't you take a leave of absence?" I nodded and from there drove directly to the cemetery. Placing a blanket on the ground, I lay on top of Marshall's grave until it was time to get James from school.

On May 3, I again called Dick to ask if he'd read John's e-mail. He said that yes, he had, but it didn't make any difference. I said, "Marshall left you a gift. He left you a $50,000 life insurance policy. He *gave* this to you. Do something good with it, Dick. He loved us both so much, and you *know* he would hate to see us fighting each other!"

He said, "I'm jealous of John and James. I have nothing left."

I said, "Can we at least drive up and talk to you personally please?"

"No," he said. "I'm sorry."

Funny, but I wasn't angry at Dick anymore for what he was putting us through. I was just incredibly sad. It was a profound sadness that just enveloped me. I could feel the weight of it pressing down, crushing me. I wanted to run away. If it weren't for James, I would have. I thought the sadness could destroy me if I let it.

On May 21, I met with the attorneys regarding settlement of Marshall's estate. We discussed the lawsuit brought against us for wrongful death.

The next day my friend Michelle recommended an organization, nationalshareoffice.com, where I could order a memorial brick to honor Marshall. There is an Angel of Hope monument in the nearby Blanchette Park in remembrance of the children and all those who have lost children. My mom and I visited the monument and were overwhelmed by the serene beauty of it. Every year in December, a candlelight service is held in honor of those children. Everyone is invited to lay a white flower at the statue's base. The brick could have up to three lines and each line could accommodate fifteen characters. We chose:

> Marshall Fink
> Beautiful One
> We Adore You

The Angel of Hope Brick Dedication was scheduled for Sunday, November 2, 2008.

The lawsuit was levied against our homeowner's policy. I had to meet with Laura B. from American Family Insurance Legal department on June 13, 2008, to give her a taped statement. It was all too much. I was still grieving for the loss of my beautiful, beloved son. But then to be blamed for that death was the ultimate blow.

I paced around the conference table while relaying all the events that led up to Marshall's death. The emotion it evokes to relive that night makes it impossible to sit still. I had done this before for the police. I had done this before for the prosecuting attorney, the reporter, and I was doing it again. My heart raced and my voice shook as I gave the details, starting from the date when I received the call from the naval hospital in 2005. Ms. B. sat there, motionless, at times looking rather stunned. When I finished, she told me that we'd be hearing from her soon. She said that the entire legal department would have to review my tape.

Dr. Simo and his staff donated a tree in Marshall's name, and it was planted in the beautiful Forest Park on June 27. My brother Alan was in town, and the five of us drove downtown to see it. I took along two gallons of spring water that had been treated with root stimulator. It's a beautiful sweet gum tree directly in front of the jewel box and just a stone's throw from the St. Louis Hills Neighborhood that Marshall loved—perfect.

On July 15, 2008, we received a letter from our insurance company:

> *Dear Mr. and Mrs. Gentles,*
>
> *We have completed our coverage investigation of the loss occurring on January 11, 2008.*
>
> *We regret to inform you there is no coverage for the loss under your policy with us.*
>
> *We will not cover bodily injury or property damage caused intentionally by or at the direction of any insured, even if the actual bodily injury or property damage is different than that which was expected or intended from the standpoint of any insured.*
>
> *We will not cover bodily injury to any insured or other person, other than a domestic employee, regularly residing on any part of the insured premises.*

> *Based on the above exclusions, we must respectfully deny any claim for damages arising from this loss.*
> *Sincerely,*
> *Casualty Claim Desk Senior Adjustor*

And so, that was that. Dick would not be receiving a settlement from our insurance company after all. I was relieved, yes, but not as much as one would expect. There was no cause for celebration, and I didn't consider it a victory. I knew that it was never really about the money. He felt guilty for letting Marshall down and wanted vindication, that's all. I knew he was going to hold on to his pain. It's the guilt that gets you. I feel it every time I visit Marshall's grave. I should have done more.

8/1/08 Heather and her boyfriend were in town, and we went out for dinner. It was an enjoyable night, and she and I stayed up late talking about Marshall. Heather said she remembered how sad Marshall looked when she and her girlfriends were saying good-bye to him in the garage on December 15th. He had been showing them his car and motorcycles, and she said that you could see he didn't want her to go. And the evening before, when she went into her bedroom, he just stayed in his room. She said he always used to go into her room so they could talk. She chose not to bother him and regrets it to this day. We sat in Marshall's closet and opened an old box of his stuffed animals. I saw his Koosa and can vividly remember him calling for this at bedtime as a child.

Afterward I became so melancholy, I started to cry softly in bed. I could hear that John wasn't asleep so I told him that I was just so sad, and no one knew how sad I really was. Then he told me how sorry he was, and I could hear him fighting back his own sobs. I said I was sorry to disturb him and that I pray every night, giving thanks. I told John, "I'm so fortunate for all I have, and I should be grateful and happy."

This comment made John blurt out, "Oh, God." He tried to console me by rubbing my back and holding me, but I was inconsolable and only fell asleep from sheer exhaustion.

When John left for work, I apologized for keeping him up. He caught his breath and said, "No, don't apologize." And we professed our love for each other.

By September 1, it had been well over six months since Marshall's death, and yet the sadness was always present. We went out with friends and had fun, but it was a momentary distraction; an escape for a little while. I remember meeting a group of friends at a bar to listen to Greg's band. I was dancing and acting carefree, but when we returned home, the silence was deafening. On several occasions, after John left for work and James went to school, I laid on the sofa, feeling a quivering sensation in my brain. I stayed there until it was time to pick up James.

On September 9, 2008 I wrote on my notepad: "Still cannot sleep. I feel dizzy, shaky, disoriented, and nauseated." And each morning I was completely and utterly exhausted. The following day I went in for another sleep study, this time at Washington University.

Impressions:
- Post-Traumatic Stress Disorder, leg movements, problem initiating sleep, maladaptive to noise (acute)
- Feritin (iron) low, causing sleep issues and leg movements.
- Recommendations:

- Take an additional 150 mg iron tablet twice daily. Retest iron in six weeks.
- No coffee or tea. They contain Tannens which interfere with iron absorption
- Drink orange juice for vitamin C

This would prove to be my last doctor visit. Truth be told, I'd lost count of all the doctor appointments I'd had since those first symptoms appeared, coinciding with Marshall's diagnosis of bipolar disorder. The iron supplement did seem to help me sleep better, which was a relief.

    By October, my calls to Dick were less frequent. Sadly, we just didn't have that much to say to one another. He always sounded down in the dumps. I encouraged him to try and triumph over his grief. I coached him to become a mentor to his niece and nephew and get involved in his church. I was worried for his well-being. He said, "Nothing really matters anymore." I told him he just wasn't trying hard enough, and that as hard as it was to lose Marshall, he's in a better place. I said God has him now. I told him that life on this earth is a blink compared to eternity in heaven and stated, "You know this is true!"

    On November 2, 2008, James and I went to Blanchette Park for the brick dedication ceremony. There were dozens of people there. Many had attended year after year, as I noticed them looking at their child's weathered bricks. I didn't know what to expect. Everyone was given a white rose to place at the base of the Angel of Hope. There was a reading, "Remember Me" by Rose Carlson and a reading of the brick description, but nothing prepared me for what came next. They played a recording of Josh Grobin singing "To Where You Are." I'd never heard this song before, and he started with: "Who can say for certain, maybe you're still here, I feel you all around me, your memory's so clear, deep within the stillness, I can hear you speak, you're still my inspiration…"

This evoked such strong emotion that I literally choked and started to openly cry. I felt raw and vulnerable. I could not contain this intense feeling and tried to hide my face. James looked miserable, too. I did not think I'd get through that song and practically sprinted to the car when it was over.

By March 9, I made the decision not to resume my employment with Dr. Simo, where I would always be reminded of my loss. The dark, isolated room would not be my friend. I needed to be in a bright, cheery environment.

On June 5, 2010 I drove up St. Charles, Illinois, to visit my sister Pat. Previously and immediately after Dick's death, on April 7, 2010 I asked his niece Amy, who was his sole heir now, if I could have two items:

- The Flag that draped Marshall's casket
- Some of Dick's ashes (I had a plan for them)

She graciously complied, and I stopped off at her house to pick them up. The flag that I had given to Dick was now mine to treasure.

On Father's Day, June 20, 2010, I went to Jefferson Barrack's Cemetery. I placed flowers by Marshall's headstone and used a trowel to dig a hole on top of his grave. I poured Dick's ashes into the earth and filled it back in, carefully replacing the sod. And now, father and son were reunited on earth as they were in heaven. Dick made it to Jefferson Barrack's to see his son's grave after all.

LETTING GO

I consciously try to push all the negative energy away, focusing only on positives and rebuilding. I will not allow self-pity. And I repeat nightly what Pastor Schlie told James's confirmation class:

"Father, thank you for sending your son Jesus who died for my sins. Thank you for loving me so much. I am reminded of your love and sacrifice every day! Thank you, Lord, for this good life, and forgive me when I don't love it enough."

Someday, I will pick up where I left off and go up against the naval council. For now, I'm content to enjoy the peace and quiet and remember the son I loved so dearly.

EPILOGUE

I continue to do research on bipolar disorder. There was an excellent interview on CBS.com with Maria Oquendo, MD who is a Professor of Clinical Psychiatry at Columbia University. She outlines the manifestations of the disorder stating the patient does not perceive their symptoms as being abnormal or anything that requires attention. She states that treatment for bipolar disorder is very different than for depression. In bipolar it is absolutely critical that the person be treated with a mood stabilizer even if they are currently depressed. If you put a patient with bipolar disorder on an anti-depressant alone, there is a risk for triggering a manic episode or a hypo-manic episode. She explains the role of the family as being absolutely critical. She speaks to family members about symptoms as they may not be apparent to the patient.

Another article titled "Health, bipolar and the wrestling industry" links steroid abuse to inducing severe mood swings and severe manic episodes in individuals who consume it. Scientific reports suggest that the testosterone patch and dihydroepiandosterone (DHEA), used as a nutritional supplement and available in health food stores, induces manic episodes and aggravates the same among bipolar patients.

An article dated April 3, 2010 in Psychiatry Magazine titled "Fish and Dietary Supplements for Bipolar Disorder" reads:

> Intake of fish and dietary supplements containing fish products which contain docosahexaenoic acid (DHA) and omega-3-fatty

acids were reported to reduce they symptoms of bipolar disorder. Last but not least, habits such as cigarette smoking, which increase cholesterol and predispose a person to cardiovascular disease are also reported to cause bipolar disorders.